Red Carpet for Mamie

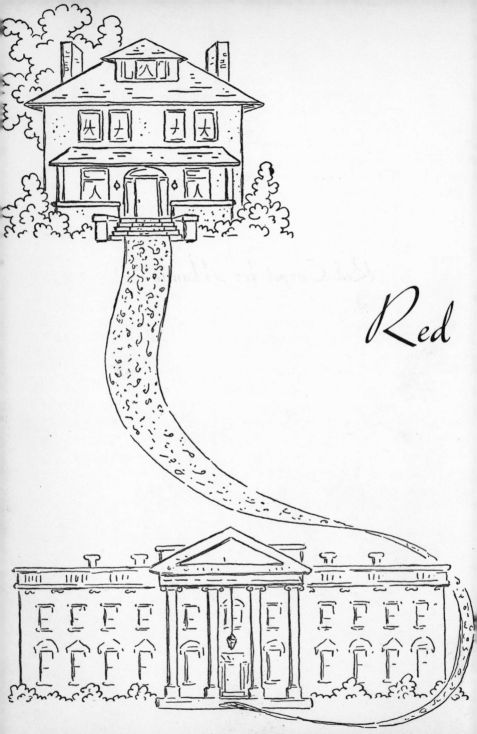

Red

Illustrations by Allene Gaty

Carpet for Mamie

by Alden Hatch

Henry Holt and Company · New York

Acknowledgments

PRIMARILY THIS BOOK IS BASED ON THE MANY STORIES I
have heard during a long, delightful friendship with the
President and Mrs. Eisenhower. Also, I was present on
quite a few occasions described in the latter part of the
book. There were, of course, numerous notes taken during my research for *General Ike,* my biography of President Eisenhower. In the course of that work I visited
Abilene, Kansas; St. Louis, Missouri; Fort Sam Houston; West Point; and Denison, Texas. In addition I spent
many days in Washington talking with General Eisenhower's friends in the Pentagon, officials of the United
States government, Presidente Sergio Osmeña of the
Philippines, etc., and working with Mrs. Eisenhower in
her apartment at the Wardman Park Hotel. To the scores
of people who helped me in all those places I repeat the
thanks I have already given them in *General Ike.*

My research for *Red Carpet for Mamie* took me frequently to Washington where I talked with Mrs. Eisenhower at the White House as well as with her friends in that city. I also went to Gettysburg and twice to Denver, where I met and talked with many of Mrs. Eisenhower's schoolmates, teachers, former beaux, and lifelong friends. In this connection I want especially to express my appreciation to Mrs. Eisenhower's mother, Mrs. John Sheldon Doud and to her sister, Mrs. George Gordon Moore.

Others to whom I owe much gratitude for their assistance include: Mr. and Mrs. Robert F. Archibold, Mr. and Mrs. Edward F. Bird, Mr. John Askling, Mrs. Gustaf Askling, General and Mrs. Arthur Nevins, Mrs. John W. Walker, Mrs. J. W. Helms, Mr. and Mrs. Joel Carlson, Governor Dan Thornton of Colorado, Mrs. George Peck, Mr. Robert Guertler, Miss Jessie Hamilton, Mr. George Sibley, Mr. and Mrs. Russell Writer, Mr. Vance McMannus, Mr. Earl A. Paul, The Honorable and Mrs. Paul V. McNutt, Mrs. Clarence Norton Goodwin, Mr. James C. Hagerty, Mrs. Mary Jane McCaffree, Mrs. Madlyn Fitzgerald, and Mrs. Elizabeth Thorpe.

Most of all I want to thank the President and Mrs. Eisenhower for the honor of their friendship and their many kindnesses throughout the years.

ALDEN HATCH

Contents

Red Carpet for Mamie

1

The Red Carpet

THE RED CARPET WAS THE HALLMARK OF THE DOUDS IN
Denver. It stretched down the high front stoop of their
house, making a bright splash of color that sharply dif-
ferentiated it from all the other houses on Lafayette
Street.

It was not really a carpet at all, not like those dismal
red runners that black-coated men stretch down the
church steps for a wedding or a funeral. Nor did it re-
semble the plush purplish strips that protect the feet of
royalty from the pavement. It was, in fact, a small rectangular rug with a pattern of green leaves, which was
hardly noticeable against its deep red background. But
everybody in Denver called it the red carpet.

Somehow it was typical of the Douds, who always did
things with a certain dash; they had the quality that the
French call *le panache*—the white plume.

In other respects the outside of their house was not remarkable. It was built of cream-color brick in a four-square, unimaginative fashion that had no particular architectural style. It was the Douds themselves who made it such a special place to be that all the young people who knew them gathered there.

This white plume of theirs showed up in other ways. For example, Mr. Doud loved fine cars. He always bought the biggest, newest models, all covered with gadgets of gleaming brass that literally knocked your eye out when they caught the strong sunlight of the Mile High City. Mrs. Doud had an electric coupé that was like a beautiful glass cabinet on wheels. It was lined with dark blue silk upholstery like a jewel box. The Doud girls called it "Creepy," because it moved so slowly, but they knew its worth as a showcase.

Then there was "Tall and Stately Jack," the Douds' Negro butler, who had the proud bearing of an Indian sachem; and there was the basement playroom, the first in Denver and perhaps in all the Mountain States. In it was a pool table. Some of the more conservative Denverites thought it was a little fast of the Douds to play pool so much.

All these things together showed the high-hearted way of the Doud family. At the same time they each served a purpose. In that land of great distances the utility of a fine automobile is obvious, and for short runs in traffic that was still mainly horse-drawn, Creepy was a great convenience for them. Jack was not only an ornamental figure, but a very handy man around the house, who doubled in brass as chauffeur. The playroom helped to make the Douds' home the center for the younger crowd, which they considered preferable to having their daughters gadding all over town.

Finally, the basic purpose of the red carpet was also utilitarian. The six shallow steps that led down from the front porch to the terrace on which the house was perched were a wonderful place to sit and observe the pleasant, slow-moving flow of life along Lafayette Street. But being made of stone, they were hard and cold on small feminine bottoms. Hence, Mrs. Doud decreed that the carpet should be spread over them on all fine days. That it was also rather "snarky" did not displease her.

On a warm evening forty years ago—almost any evening of any summer at that time—Mamie Doud would be sitting on the top step with half a dozen young men looking up at her with various degrees of adoration. Some of them were desperately in love with her; others were there merely to enjoy her beauty and charm. For Mamie was a very pretty girl.

It is hard to give an accurate picture of her as she sat there, because there were so many contradictions that all added up to Mamie. For example, she was not technically beautiful; her nose was a millimeter too long, her mouth too generous, and her shining brown hair swirled down her high forehead in a curious untamed style of her own. On the other hand, her long-lashed eyes were the dark blue of a piece of sky reflected in a well, and her skin seemed actually translucent, so fair and delicate was it. Now there lies another contradiction. Mamie was dainty and, at the same time, hearty, with the warm earthiness of the people of the western plains and mountains. She was restful to be with, yet her enthusiasm for life was expressed in constant movement, so that she rippled in the breeze of her own excitement.

She was rather vain, yet most thoughtful of other people, especially older ones. She was demure, but a complete extrovert who loved to show off. When she laughed, which was often, she laughed down deep, and the sound

of it echoed up the street for a couple of blocks at least. She was a romantic flirt, yet she fell in love only once— and forever!

Inevitably, she had a great many beaux. In those days the modern business of pairing off, of "going steady," had not come into fashion. Each pretty girl had a string of young men at her command, and the men often paid attention to more than one girl. The pairing off came later and was for keeps.

Most of Mamie's young men played some sort of

musical instrument—mandolins, banjos, or the highly romantic guitar. Vance McMannus played the trumpet professionally in the Denver band, but that was not very suitable for serenading, so he got up a very good quartet. When they all gathered on the Douds' steps, somebody was sure to start singing. The others would pick up the refrain, and sure enough, before long Mamie's high, sweet voice joined, mingled, and soared above the others, carrying up and down that quiet street, where nearly everybody knew everybody else, so that people sitting on their vine-screened porches as far up as Eighth Avenue cocked their ears and smiled and said, "Mamie's enjoying herself."

When they tired of singing, they talked quietly in the strong cool air that flowed down from the mountains at that hour every evening. The young men were warmed by the knowledge that though Mamie might not love them, she liked them all enormously. For that was her special characteristic—liking people so much that her warmth flowed over them, and embraced them, and made them feel welcome and happy.

That is the picture people in Denver still hold in memory's eye of Lafayette Street forty years ago.

If this were a moving picture instead of a book, there would now be what Hollywood calls a montage—a succession of brief flashes to indicate the passage of years. There would indubitably be the stock shot of a calendar with its leaves flying off, a few clips of men in trenches, Herbert Hoover getting inaugurated, a jet plane swooping down on Korea, and a dissolve of the Douds' wonderful old Winton Six turning into a streamlined Cadillac.

Then the camera would pick up the Douds' red carpet in the election year of 1952. At a distance it would look almost the same. Mamie was sitting there holding court, and men were lounging on the steps in various degrees of admiration. But as the camera moved in from "long shot" to "medium close-up," you would notice first the difference in clothes. Instead of tight-fitting dark suits with high collars or striped blazers, ice-cream pants, and pie-plate straw hats, the men wore gaudy sport shirts or light-colored summer suits of synthetic silks. Mamie had changed her flowing, toe-touching organdie gown for a short-skirted print. Then you would see that they all looked a good deal older. There were tiny wrinkles around Mamie's lovely eyes, and many of her admirers had white hair or none at all. Their faces were eroded by work and worry and service to their country into deep lines and craggy ridges. The beauty and some of the grace of youth were gone forever, though character and distinction in some measure might have replaced them.

So everything seemed changed. These men sitting on the old front stoop were the political leaders of their states, newspaper men with columns that millions read and pondered, leaders of industry and finance, of farmers and miners and factory hands. Most of them were Republicans come to help their candidate get nominated and elected, but a large minority had come to find out what kind of folk these Eisenhowers really were, to see if they deserved the confidence of their country. They were desperately serious about it. For whatever may be written about the dickering and deals and general shenanigans in politics, there is at bottom a firm base of integrity. The men in whom the American people place their confidence, who have the awful power to sway public opinion, are conscious that this is perhaps the most sacred trust of all. With a few lamentable exceptions, they really try their hardest to be worthy of this trust, and they therefore examine a presidential candidate with the microscopic suspicion of a scientist identifying a new virus.

They are even more suspicious of the candidate's wife, for Presidents have been made or wrecked by their wives; and often very little is known about the distaff side of a presidential team until the lady bursts upon a startled nation from the White House.

So the men who came to call on Mamie that critical summer were not there for relaxation or sociability. Indeed, they were tense with anxiety, asking the vital question, would she measure up?

Mamie was perfectly well aware of their mental reservations. She was also conscious that she knew very little about the world of politics, having been insulated from it most of her life by the curious code, which, until recently, forbade career soldiers from taking any part in the government of the United States. Mamie loyally wanted to help Ike serve his country, but she did not know what techniques and subtleties and flatteries to use. So she decided just to be herself.

She sat on the red carpet, and the great men came from all the forty-eight states to sit on the steps and talk to her. At first they were stiff and she was uneasy. Then she discovered that they were wonderful people and that she liked them enormously, so her spontaneous warmth flowed out and enveloped them, and they forgot to be wary and difficult. They began to relax in the feeling of being liked for themselves alone. Pretty soon they were making little jokes that made Mamie's uninhibited laughter ring out so that people 'way up at Eighth Avenue heard it and smiled in sympathy.

Thus things were not so different after all from the way they had been in the summertime long ago—except that what had happened during those forty years had made what was happening now on the Douds' red carpet very important for America and, in fact, for the whole world.

2

Family Portrait

MAMIE GENEVA DOUD WAS BORN IN BOONE, IOWA, ON November 14, 1896. A pin stuck in the center of a map of the North American continent would come fairly close to hitting Boone. The little city stands surrounded by the flat, luxuriant fields of grain and grass that are the heartland of America.

From an airplane flying over it one can see the rectangular pattern that the pioneers laid out. The ruler-straight, brown roads, which divide the fields, run exactly east and west or north and south, following the meridians of longitude and parallels of latitude along which some lonely surveyor plowed a furrow through the prairie sod to mark off the sections and quarter sections. This immense agricultural checkerboard stretches for hundreds of miles in all directions to the hazy horizon. Cities, towns, and villages show as more crowded, but equally formal, gridirons. Only the silver rivers, looping and twisting through the plain, break the pattern with delightfully inconsequential abandon.

The John Sheldon Douds lived in a bungalow on the edge of Boone. On one side of it the street ran down to the business district and on to the Carlson grain elevators and flour mill and the Doud meat-packing plant. On the other side wide fields of stubble bleakly were beginning their winter's rest.

The Douds were a handsome young couple. Though he was of English descent and her parents had been born in Sweden, they looked surprisingly alike. Doud was a tall, powerful man of thirty-one, with gray eyes, strong features and a ruddy skin. Elivera Carlson Doud was tall, too, slender but big-framed. With her wheat-gold hair, deep blue eyes, and fair complexion she looked like a Norse goddess. Though she was just eighteen, she had been married for two years, and this would be her second child.

The weather was at its worst that November day. Rain, driven by a northeast wind, slashed against the one-story frame house and seeped through the window sashes. John Doud, who had taken the day off, alternately stoked the Franklin stove in the parlor, the wood-burning kitchen range, and the fire in his young wife's room, so the house kept snug enough, though it was a little chilly at the edges.

The small rooms seemed quite crowded. Elivera Doud's mother, Mrs. Carl Carlson, was there; and her sister, Eda Wilhelmina, chattering in Swedish, which all the Carlsons spoke at home. The Doud's first baby, Eleanor, who was just a year old, seemed imbued with the general excitement. She refused to take her midday nap, and kept climbing out of her wooden Swedish cradle and crawling under everyone's feet. Finally the family doctor came. He wore a beard and looked imposing in the black swallowtail coat that was almost the uniform of his profession. Marking the equatorial region of his paunch was a massive gold watch chain from which an onyx seal and a big gold key jingled as he bent to examine the young mother.

The baby was born at two o'clock in the afternoon. She was tiny, and the few wisps of hair that showed on her wrinkled scalp were brown. When she finally opened her eyes, they appeared to be so deep a blue that in some lights they were violet. Everyone said, "Of course they'll turn brown as she gets older." But, as so often happens, everyone was wrong.

Despite his relief that his dear wife's ordeal was over and the baby was healthy and howled with promising volume, John Doud was secretly and deeply disappointed. The Douds were very proud of their name and the vigor of their family. John Doud had hoped so much that this child would be a son.

Mamie Doud's birthplace was in mid-America, and her ancestry was typical of her country. The Douds were as English as the Magna Carta. They had come to America 250 years before. The Carlsons were Swedish, the first generation in the land, but no less American for that. The first Doud of record was Henry Doude of Guildford, in the County of Surrey, who embarked in the great adventure of seventeenth-century Englishmen, a voyage to the colonies. Behind him stand shadowy figures said to have been country gentlemen with manor houses and a family crest. All that is merely legend.

Fact begins when Henry Doude landed on the forested coast of Connecticut in 1639. Even the little wooden towns in their clearings among the great trees must have seemed too cramped for him, since he moved on with a small group of kindred spirits to found a village of his own. He named it Guildford, after his home town. That was in 1648.

Whether aristocrats or not, the Douds—they soon dropped that unessential e—brought with them the British principle of primogeniture. In their family the eldest son inherited everything; the others moved on westward to found their own fortunes.

By the early eighteen hundreds the Douds had gone as far as Rome, New York, beside the newly built Erie Canal. Along it moved a steady stream of canal boats, laden with the produce of the new Midwestern states and the manufactured articles from the East. Settlers by the thousands passed through, heading west in the gaily painted canal packets, each drawn by its three-horse hitch and progressing at the strictly enforced speed limit of four miles an hour.

Until the railroads took the traffic away from the "canawlers," Rome was an important junction point, a good place to build a business. Mamie's grandfather, Royal Houghton Doud, laid the pediment of the family fortune by founding the wholesale grocery firm of Foote, Doud and Company. It did very nicely for a while, but Doud, who was as restless as he was energetic, saw that Rome was withering on the vine when the steam cars passed it by. He sold out and headed for Chicago, the center of the railroad net that was rapidly spreading over the whole continent. There he went into the sure-fire business of meat packing, founding the R. H. Doud Company with his brother Eli in 1877.

By 1895 Royal Doud had made his pile and retired. But even in his sixties he was no man to sit on a porch, whittling. A couple of years of idleness were more than enough for him. He opened his Chicago *Tribune* one morning and read in black, smashing headlines of the gold strike on the Yukon. His foot began to itch; the call of adventure burned like ichor in his veins. Neither the pleas of his wife nor the warnings of his friends could stop him. With the impetuosity of a sixteen-year-old he headed for Alaska.

But he fancied himself too astute to seek the chimera of gold. Let other men play the heartbreaking game of prospecting those ice-bound crags and gorges. He proposed to trade with the lucky few who hit pay dirt, to make another fortune in secondhand gold dust. Not that he needed it, or even wanted it. He really played the game for the sake of playing.

That time he lost. Though he was right in principle— great fortunes were made supplying the prospectors' needs—he was wrong in particular. Cannily, as he thought, he took along many crates of candles. He reached the end of the long bitter trail to the gold fields in May, 1898. To his dismay he found that on the rim of the Arctic Circle the days of spring were 23 hours long. The one thing nobody needed in Dawson City was a candle!

Financially bent and physically broken, Royal Doud came home from his last adventure. He died in the autumn of 1899.

John Sheldon Doud, Royal Doud's son and Mamie's father, was unquestionably a chip off the sturdy Doud block. He was born in Rome and was six years old when the family moved to Chicago. Before he was eighteen he ran away from home three times. The first time he did not get far. He and a Jewish boy, who was his best friend, hoboed their way to South Bend, Indiana, before homesickness turned the cream of adventure sour. Their retreat to home and mother was hasty.

The next summer, when John Doud set off alone, he traveled faster and farther. He made his way to the Mississippi, riding the rods underneath a string of empty cattle cars. The train was hitched together by pin-and-chain couplings with plenty of play. Every time the engineer put on the brakes, all the cars banged into each other with a series of shattering jolts. Doud had to hang on like a monkey in a typhoon to keep from being thrown to the rails and minced by the flanged wheels.

When he got to the river, Doud traveled more luxuriously, stowing away in a stern-wheel steamboat that looked a little like a three-tiered wedding cake with her ornate white and gold superstructure. From his hiding place among the barrels on the forward deck, he could hear the hiss of her bows parting the muddy water and see the steersman in the pilothouse far above him, spinning her great mahogany wheel as he deftly avoided the snags and sand bars of the shifting channel. Tall twin smokestacks trailed black smoke by day. At night streams of golden sparks swirled out of them like fiery serpents in the sky.

Doud debarked inconspicuously at Memphis, Tennessee, and looked for work—any work. He was unusually big and strong for his age, so the foreman of a gang of laborers hired him to work on the levee. You can't keep a good Doud down. John soon earned his just promotion—to third cook for the outfit.

His day began at 3:30 A.M., when he crawled out of his shack behind the levee and set about getting an enormous breakfast for the gang. It ended 15 hours later when the last pick-wielding Irishman had wolfed down his supper of Mulligan stew. At that, it was easier than working the standard 12-hour day, toting sandbags with the thermometer registering 120 degrees in the sun.

John Doud held the job three months and proved himself to his own satisfaction. Back in Chicago his family wondered where he was, but they did not call the police and send out a six-state alarm. They were confident he could take care of himself.

John Doud had one more fling, a comparatively short jaunt to Council Bluffs, Iowa. After that he decided that he wanted an education and settled down to study at the University of Chicago. He duly was graduated. Then, for practical education, he took a job in the stockyards at Omaha. Thus he returned to the mainstream of the family enterprise with his drive and energy unabated.

By the time he was twenty-eight, he had founded his own business, John S. Doud and Company, with headquarters in Boone, Iowa. The firm was in the livestock commission business and was closely allied with his brother Jim's Chicago house, the J. M. Doud Company, and with the original meat-packing company. With his business prospering and his future assured, it was time to think of marriage and a family of his own.

The Carlson's family name was not Carlson at all. It was Jeremiahson. Soon after he came to America, Mamie's grandfather changed it to Carlson because English-speaking people seemed inclined to grin when they heard it. In Sweden it had been a perfectly serious, respectable sort of name, and Carl Jeremiahson had been a serious, respectable young man. He worked as confidential messenger for a wealthy Swedish family, which was a position of trust and responsibility. Carl was married to Johanna Maria Andersen, and his career seemed plainly mapped in the sober Swedish way of neither too much nor too little, but always comfort and security. However, Carl was ambitious.

He and Johanna must have had many serious talks in their cozy little flat in Stockholm before he decided on the great gamble of coming to America. It took much courage on his part to make the decision, and even more on hers to send her young husband off to that far, wild continent, where the lure of illimitable opportunity was balanced by unimaginable perils.

Carl landed from a small immigrant ship in Boston in 1868. From there he went to Canada, where he found work in a brickyard, and on to a farm in Illinois. Neither the brickyard nor the farm lived up to the golden promise of America; and, in November when the crops were in and the farm snugged down for the winter, Carl Carlson collected his small wages and started walking westward.

It was tough going. The roads were hardly more than cart tracks, sloughs of mud or deep frozen ruts. They ran due west, cutting straight across the prairie until they went off the edge of infinity. Carl walked all day, every day, and still the ribbon of road stretched on ahead as though there were no end to that rich plain.

The weather was bitterly cold. Carl did not mind that; it was the one thing that made him feel at home in this vast lonely land. But when a blizzard howled out of the northwest, driving the stinging pellets of snow against his face, swirling them in ten-foot drifts across the road, he sometimes wondered if he would survive, and thought of the big snowflakes falling softly between the forested hills of home.

Eventually he came to a small town, built of raw, unpainted wood, whose people told him it was called Montana, in the state of "Ioway." There he decided to pause a while, a resting place that became his permanent home.

That winter he earned his living cutting wood. He started out each day in the first gray light, carrying his lunch pail, which usually contained a hunk of salt pork, some cornbread, and a cup of applesauce. When he got thirsty, he chopped a hole in the ice of a frozen stream and dipped the water up in a tin cup. Other men worked with him, their axes ringing in the crisp air as they bit into the great trees that had been growing for half a thousand years.

When the sun dipped low enough to throw a rosy glare over the icebound plain beyond the belt of forest, the woodsmen loaded their logs on big bobsleds drawn by four-horse teams and rode homeward through the twilight.

Carl was a good worker and a frugal man. By April, 1869, he had saved enough money to send to Sweden for Johanna. They set up housekeeping in rented rooms. Eventually the lumber company paid Carl a sort of bonus in the form of a large frame house and lot. It had ten rooms, plenty of space for a growing family, and big shady porches. The front parlor was especially fine. It was lighted by Carl's proudest possession, a large oil lamp that hung on a cord from the ceiling. By means of a Goldbergian arrangement of pulleys, it could be raised and lowered for various purposes.

Mamie's uncle, Joel Carlson, who is vice-president of the Citizens' National Bank of Boone, lives there now. And the front parlor is still illuminated by that variable-height lamp—converted to electricity.

The Carlsons grew up with the town, which soon changed its name to Boone. Carl became manager of the new flour mill. Later he saved enough money to buy it, and he added tall grain elevators that could be seen for miles across the prairie. When his eldest son, Charles, grew up, he took him into partnership.

Elivera Mathilda Carlson was born at the time of her father's greatest happiness and prosperity. She had two brothers, Charles and Joel, and a sister, Eda Wilhelmina. Their home was like a bit of Sweden, transplanted and flourishing in the Midwest. When the family were together, they always spoke the crisp, musical language of their parents' native land.

Particularly memorable was their old-fashioned Swedish Christmas. They all got up at four o'clock in the morning for *Julotta*, the Christmas service that began at five. All over Boone lights were coming on in the houses of the many Scandinavian families, and people were hurriedly getting dressed in their best clothes. The dark and the tingling cold made it tremendously exciting. Then all the Carlsons piled into their big, two-horse sleigh. Carl cracked the whip and off they went, bells jingling, runners creaking and crunching through the crusty snow. It was so cold that the horses' breath seemed like steam spurting from a locomotive. The wooden church, with its pointed arches lighted by dozens of red candles and its pot-bellied stove glowing crimson from the roaring wood fire, seemed warm and full of the true spirit of Christmas.

After church there was an enormous dinner, planned for months ahead of time. The big table was loaded with

A.G.

such Scandinavian delicacies as lingonberries, which came from Sweden carefully packed in little wooden kegs, *sylta,* and strong native cheeses called *Kum minost* and *getost. Sill,* which was pickled herring, also came from Sweden in wooden cases.

After dinner they would sing lovely old Swedish hymns, Eda's high soprano rising above all the rest. They were a deeply religious family who had morning and evening prayer every day. Carl was a pillar of the First Evangelical Church of Boone, where he taught Sunday School.

Despite his fondness for Swedish traditions, Carlson soon became an American citizen and took a lively interest in politics. He was an ardent Republican and acquired a strong following among men of Scandinavian descent who lived in Iowa. This made him something of a power in the party. Mrs. Doud can still remember the excitement of elections—the torchlight parades with her father leading the way, his ceremonial high silk hat gleaming in the shifting light of the flares, the thump and boom of the drums, and her brothers proudly carrying a big banner that proclaimed their fervent belief in Benjamin Harrison.

Elivera Carlson was just sixteen—the right age for marrying—when John Doud came courting her. He was 13 years older than she, handsome, and established in business. According to Swedish thinking, it was a most suitable match. According to Elivera, she loved him then and all their lives. So they were married.

Another Redskin Bit the Dust

MAMIE REMEMBERS BOONE ONLY FROM VISITS TO HER grandfather and uncle. When she was seven months old, her parents moved to Cedar Rapids, Iowa. It was not much of a change. Cedar Rapids was only a little larger than Boone and, like it, was one of those small urban centers that existed mainly to serve the needs of the farmers roundabout. The Douds lived in a pleasant little house on a tree-shaded street. In that house Mamie's memories first took shape, so in a psychic sense that is where her life began.

First came the postman, a tall, genial gentleman dressed in gray, with a big worn leather sack over his shoulder and his hands full of letters. Mamie liked to greet him on the porch. He would stoop down and hand her the letters. She would thank him and bustle importantly in to her mother.

One day he seemed extra merry. "I know of a little white lamb that has just been born," he said. "It needs a home. Would anyone around here like a lamb?"

"Yes!" said Mamie, dancing with excitement.

"I suppose so," Mrs. Doud agreed dubiously from behind the screen door.

When the postman came next day, he reached into his sack and drew out a white, fuzzy object with ridiculously long legs. He set it down on the veranda, and it wobbled helplessly toward Mamie, who grabbed it up and hugged it in an excess of motherliness that almost finished it off. Soon she learned to play with it gently, and everyone was enchanted by the pretty picture they made.

However, the trouble with Mamie's little lamb was, first, that it did not stay little, and secondly, that it was an infant ram. Though a little girl could learn to play gently, sheep are less susceptible to reason. All in a spirit of fun one day, the lamb backed up about three yards, lowered its bony bullet head, and charged the most tempting target in sight. It scored a center on Mamie's round little stomach. Down she went with all the breath knocked out of her. When she got it back, her agonized howl scared the lamb into the next-door neighbor's yard and brought Eleanor and Mrs. Doud flying to the rescue. Thus was Mamie first made painfully aware of the damage unthinking friends may do.

Next came Kate, a handsome bay mare, who drew a gleaming surrey complete with the traditional fringe around the top. She became a real friend of the family and, later, a prominent personalty in the scheme of things on Lafayette Street.

Just before her sixth birthday Mamie started school. Dressed in a blue Peter Thompson, a sort of little girl's sailor suit, and with a tight grip on her mother's hand,

she started nervously into the great world of "other people." Of course, she did not have very far to go. Jackson School was directly across the street from the Douds' home; she had watched the children playing in the yard all her short life. In addition, Eleanor was already there. Nevertheless, that short walk of 50 feet was the first long step of her career, as it is for every child, her first venture on her own outside the closed circle of the family. The way she reacted would indicate something about the pattern of her whole life.

From the first, Mamie was a good pupil and a poor student. Even then she instinctively liked people and therefore wanted to please them. This made her cooperative, obedient, and reliable. When she was given a set task, such as tidying the coatroom or filling the inkwells sunk in each small desk, she carried it out neatly and conscientiously. She was popular with both teachers and pupils.

Study was another matter. Mamie was never one to take life at second hand. Books were so much duller than people that she wanted as little to do with them as possible. Though she had a quick, understanding mind, she applied it the minimal amount necessary to get by.

In an age when a rather disproportionate importance is attached to such things as B.A. or M.A. following a name, this may seem a woeful lack of initiative. Actually, it is a question whether studious application would have fitted Mamie any better for the unforeseeable role she was to play in the spotlight of the world. After all, in the Eisenhower partnership in all its phases—as the wife of a young, ambitious officer; of a great general, whose social obligations included maintaining friendly relations with the representatives of our uneasy allies; and, finally, as the wife of a politician and a President—her function was to make people feel welcome and happy. To this end, the knowledge of people and the tact and kindness which comes from within are infinitely more important than intellectual attainment.

Besides, Mamie obtained the essentials of culture more or less by osmosis. Her father and mother were cultivated people. In their house, books were familiar things and music was an absolute essential. Almost every evening Mr. Doud read aloud to his daughters. Despite her indifference to books, Mamie loved these evenings, for her father's voice made the people between the pages come alive.

The Doud family was now complete. Mamie had two younger sisters, Eda Mae, born in 1900, and Frances, born in 1902. Those were their formal names, which nobody ever used. Mr. Doud, still unreconciled to his sonless state, called them Buster and Mike. They were even dressed like boys in Buster Brown suits, which consisted of long, straight blouses with turned-down stiff collars, knee-length knickers to match, and long black stockings. Despite this treatment, Buster, with her golden hair and big blue eyes, was resolutely feminine. Mike was a tomboy all the way.

An interesting reversal was simultaneously occurring in the Eisenhower household back in Abilene, Kansas. Ike's father was so distressed by having seven sons and no daughter that he dressed Milton, the youngest, in sissy velvet suits and made him wear long corkscrew curls until he was nearly five years old.

Despite his disappointment at their persistent femininity, Mr. Doud loved his daughters dearly. He called them "my four little women," and made up all sorts of pleasant nonsense to amuse them. When they began to ask where they came from, he invented unlikely places where he had found them. According to him, Mike was discovered under a cabbage leaf and Buster in a rose bush. He teased Mamie, who was the daintiest of all, by claiming to have pulled her out of the ash can.

After the evening reading was over and the children had said their prayers, Pappa always had to tell them a good-night story. Child psychologists would blow a gasket and modern educators flip their eyebrows at the subjects he chose. It was almost always a blood-curdling tale of pioneers, cowboys, and Indians; nor were those characters yet so far in the past but what they had considerable reality to children scarcely more than a generation removed from the real thing. As a result, nightmares were not uncommon. But when Mrs. Doud intervened, and her husband tried to switch his subject to something more soothing like a fairy princess, vociferous audience demand forced him back to the savage plains.

All the stories had a set ending, which was the signal for the girls to turn out the lights and *try* to go to sleep. The sign-off was Pappa saying in resounding tones, "And so another redskin bit the dust!"

4

On Cheyenne Mountain

FOUR CHILDREN IN SIX YEARS HAD TAKEN THEIR TOLL OF
Elivera Doud's constitution. At twenty-five she began to
go into what was referred to then as a "decline." The
doctors in Cedar Rapids, who were realists before they
were home-town boosters, recommended a change from
the ferocious climate of Iowa, where the temperature
ranged all the way from 20-odd degrees below in winter
to a stifling 100 on many a summer day.

Though Mr. Doud was only thirty-six, he had made a
fortune sufficient to guarantee his comfort and even luxury for any foreseeable future. So he decided to retire
and take his wife to the bracing climate of Colorado.

The children were wild with excitement at the prospect of going to the real West, where redskins still sur-
vived in considerable numbers. There might be a chance
of seeing one bite the dust! Mrs. Doud looked forward

to any change that would enable her to shake off her miserable lassitude. Pappa, like a true Doud, was always ready for adventure.

They settled first at Pueblo, Colorado, but soon moved on to Colorado Springs, where they rented a small house that stood in the shadow of the Frontal Range of the Rockies, which climbed almost out of the front yard to the splendid climax of Pike's Peak. The thin, crisp air at 7,000 feet soon restored Elivera Doud's natural vigor. But the great altitude had a tragic consequence for the family.

Almost the first thing Mr. Doud did in Colorado Springs was to buy a Rambler touring car with a small round hood over its four-cylinder engine and a high, seven-passenger tonneau, sheltered by a great, flapping, black top, braced and stayed against the wind by leather straps fastened to the front springs. The Rambler was capable of carrying the entire Doud family, an absolutely essential chauffeur, and a guest or two, if necessary, at a top speed of 40 miles an hour.

Since it was one of the first cars in Colorado Springs, its operation was definitely a pioneering enterprise. There were no gas stations, no garages, no mechanics, none of the modern network of services to maintain it. The roads were tortuous cowpaths wandering uncertainly through that perpendicular terrain. To reach a given destination in it was remarkable; to return home, a miracle.

Mamie liked the excitement of riding in the car with the stiff, cool wind in her face—there was no windshield. It was less enthralling when they got behind a four-mule-power wagon piled with sacks of grain, and ground along in low gear for miles. By the time a turnout enabled

them to pass, they were all thickly coated with powdery
dust. The fine grains sifted through layers of clothing
right down to their skins; eyes, ears, and noses were
clogged with it. Everybody had to take a bath after the
ride.

She thought that it was really more fun to retrogress
than to progress—to go back to the most primitive form
of mountain transportation. One livery stable at the
Springs had a corral full of burros. Their basic function
was to carry food up the mountains to prospectors working in the area of the Golden Cycle Mine. On the return
trip they were laden with samples of ore optimistically
consigned to the Assay Office. However, there were more
burros than miners, and they could be hired for excursions up Cheyenne Mountain.

One such expedition consisted of Mr. Doud, Grandpa Carlson, in black broadcloth and a square derby hat, Eleanor and Mamie in their Peter Thompsons. Mamie was riding her favorite burro, a Roman-nosed animal with ears nearly a foot long, who bore a gallant name— Geronimo!

The first stage of the trail was easy. The beasts were fresh and trotted gaily two abreast up the gentle slope. Then the acclivity grew steeper; the trail narrowed, and the footing seemed precarious with loose stones and gravel. This did not bother the burros, who scrambled upward, in single file now, with Pappa leading and Grandpa Carlson bringing up the rear to make sure nobody got left behind. In places the trail was cut into the side of the mountain. On one hand was sheer red rock; on the other, a vertiginous drop of a thousand feet or more to the rocky bed of a dry ravine. It did not worry Mamie, for she had complete confidence in Geronimo, and could look down into the abyss with the serene indifference of total security.

When they reached the top a splendid prospect opened out. To the east, in all the pastel shades of agriculture from mauve to palest yellow, the vast plains sloped imperceptibly away to an infinitely distant horizon. Westward was the violence of the mountains, ridge topping soaring ridge, forever icy peaks tossed upward against the sky like the waves of a monstrous ocean petrified at the climactic center of a hurricane.

Though they had seen it before, they all sat silent for a moment. Even the children were slightly stunned by the grandeur of that fabulous panorama. Then Mamie broke the silence. "I'm hungry," she said.

Mrs. Doud, who had remained home with the younger

children, had foreseen this contingency. Pappa was provided with a bulging picnic basket. They camped on a flat outcrop of rock. The sun, blazing down through the thin veil of atmosphere at 9,000 feet, was wonderfully hot, though in the shade the wind had the sharp edge of winter.

Following good Western custom, they gave the animals first helpings. Saddle girths were eased and nosebags full of oats were adjusted over upstanding ears. Then the wonders of the picnic basket were unwrapped. There were thick roast-beef sandwiches, hard-boiled eggs, and a new-fangled thermos bottle full of cold milk. For dessert there were more sandwiches spread with yellow country butter and strawberry jam, and big wedges of chocolate layer cake wrapped in oiled paper.

Mamie ate with the gusto of a newsboy at a free turkey dinner. She wolfed her sandwiches, with red juice making little furrows through the dust on her chin. Eleanor languidly picked at a hard-boiled egg and offered her sister the remains of a half-eaten sandwich.

"Don't you really want it?" Mamie asked, eyeing it greedily.

"I truly don't," Eleanor said. "I'm not very hungry."

Mr. Doud looked up at her keenly. "Don't you feel well, Eleanor?" he asked anxiously.

"I'm all right, Pappa," she said. "It's just that I've got a little pain. Perhaps I drank my milk too fast. I was so thirsty."

"That's probably it," her father agreed. But he was not quite satisfied. It was not like Eleanor to feel sick.

On the way back, however, she seemed to get steadily better, and by the time they got down to level ground, she was ready to bet Mamie that her burro could beat Geronimo back to the stables.

Then there was another day on the mountain and another race. That time Mrs. Doud was along and they went to the Cheyenne Monument. As they stood looking up at it, Eleanor asked, "How many steps are there?"

"Three hundred and sixty-five," Mrs. Doud answered. "One for every day in the year."

"Bet I could go up it without even stopping," said Eleanor. "Do you think you could, Mamie?"

"Sure," said Mamie. "Let's try!"

"It's a foolish—" began Mrs. Doud. But the two little girls were already scampering up the long cascade of steps. Their mother watched them a little anxiously as they seemed to get smaller and smaller as they neared the top. They were not running now. Even at that distance she could see them laboring, but they did not stop.

"Rest a while," she called. But they went doggedly on.

Eleanor won her bet; she never stopped until she reached the top. Mamie, who was close behind her, saw Eleanor force herself up the last step of all. Then she collapsed on the ground. She was as gray as granite and gasping for breath. "I've got a pain in my side," she sobbed. "It hurts awful. . . ."

Seeing Eleanor writhing on the ground above, and Mamie making pathetically frantic gestures for help, Mr. Doud also went up the steps without stopping. He was really frightened when he saw Eleanor's agony, but he pretended to be calm. "You've got a stitch in your side," he said. "It will go away pretty soon."

Then he gathered her up in his strong, comforting arms and carried her down from Calvary.

5

Mile–High City

THE DOCTOR LOOKED VERY SERIOUS WHEN HE HAD EX-
amined Eleanor. She was suffering from a severe heart
attack. He explained to her anxious father and mother
that some people's bodies could not adjust to the thin
air above 7,000 feet. Eleanor's heart, already weakened
by the altitude, had been seriously damaged by the
enormous strain which her indomitable spirit had put
upon it by climbing that long flight of steps. She must
remain absolutely quiet in bed for the present. For the
long pull he urgently advised the Douds to move to a
somewhat lower region. Denver, he suggested, at nearly
2,000 feet less altitude, would be a good place.

Mr. Doud immediately took a train to Denver and
found a temporary home for them at 101 North Logan
Street. As soon as Eleanor was well enough to travel, the
whole family moved there. Eleanor showed immediate

improvement. Mr. and Mrs. Doud were so delighted with Denver that they decided to make it their home.

The first thing was to find a permanent place to live. The Douds went house hunting in their new Oldsmobile up and down the quiet shady streets of what was then the new residential section of the city. An ample brick house which was just being completed at 750 Lafayette Street seemed exactly designed to meet their requirements. There were plenty of bedrooms, a big back yard for the girls to play in, and a shady front porch with a flight of broad shallow steps leading down to the terrace, and another short flight down to the pavement. Mr. Doud bought it for cash on the barrel head, and they finished and furnished it to their own taste. As it was on the day the Douds moved in, so it is, almost exactly, today. Once the colors were chosen and the furniture arranged, Mr. Doud would allow nothing to be changed. "If I come home in the dark some night," he said, "I want to know exactly where everything is and not go stumbling around."

Solid and *substantial* are inescapable words in describing the home where Mamie grew up. Add *comfort*, and there it is. The hall had dark, oak wainscotting and heavy oak furniture; a short flight of stairs led to a broad landing with a table and lamp and a severe, oaken grandfather's clock. In one corner of the hall was a fireplace of dark red brick. The front parlor was small but —again an inevitable word—*elegant*. Grouped around the little fireplace of off-white tile with a rosewood mantel were mahogany and rosewood chairs upholstered in petit point, each with its small petit-point footstool. On the table between the windows stood a large French clock in the Greek revival style, small Corinthian pillars supporting its glass-sided case, a bronze lion crouching on top. Family photographs and miniatures crowded tables and mantel, *bibelots* were in cabinets and on shelves, and, lest the world see in, lace curtains at all the windows. The dining room, with a bay window overlooking the back yard, was the brightest room. There were a buffet with the massive Doud silver and cabinets with shelf after shelf of sparkling cut glass. The round, mahogany dining table still bears the scars of small scuffing shoes on its claw-and-ball feet, because Mr. Doud, the old sentimentalist, would never allow it to be refinished.

The Douds really had fun fixing up the playroom in the cellar—"the wreck room," Mrs. Doud called it. No attempt was made to disguise the fat hot water pipes that crossed its ceiling; they were simply painted gold, giving a futuristic look to a room that was well in advance of its time.

The massive pool table inevitably was its main feature. Racks for balls and cues hung beside it, and little disks of wood were strung on a wire for scoring the game. An antelope head with thin, curving horns looked crossly down on the pool players. A big, black leather club chair was where Mr. Doud sat when he was not playing. At the other end of the room was a brick fireplace and, later, a green baize poker table. The little upright piano with which the Douds started housekeeping stood against one wall, and an early, wax-cylinder phonograph with a flowerlike trumpet was on a table. As time passed and the genius of others improved Mr. Edison's invention, this was replaced by the latest models.

There was a sort of closet kitchen beside the stairs with a two-burner gas stove where the girls practiced cooking and made fudge and midnight snacks. By way of decoration it had an oval lithograph of a merry street urchin whispering something in his companion's ear. Its title was "A Quiet Tip," and, underneath, the legend read: "Confide Your Live Stock to The J. M. Doud Company Union Stock Yards, Chicago." Hanging it was a nice bit of bravado on the part of the Douds, since Denver society stuffily considered mining much more aristocratic than meat packing.

The Douds moved into their new house in 1906. It marked the end of their wanderings, though not of their travels, which are very different things. It was the sure base to which they always came back.

To Mamie, who has had to follow her husband through a bewildering variety of temporary residences—from a junior officer's two-room quarters at Fort Sam Houston through the long succession of Army posts, varied by bat-ridden tropical villas, Philippine extravagancies, apartments in Paris and Washington, a castle in Scotland, and a classical villa at Marne La Coquette to the ultimate transientness of 1600 Pennsylvania Avenue—it is still the only place she can call home.

The social scientists always are fighting about which is more influential, heredity or environment; but no one denies that both are important. Certainly the city where Mamie spent the ten formative years of her life was a powerful influence in shaping her character.

When the Douds moved to Denver in 1906, not 50 years had passed since the discovery of gold had brought prospectors, miners, and all their picturesque train of gamblers, badmen, and burlesque queens pouring into the enormous, empty land of plains and mountains then known as Arapahoe County of Kansas Territory. In

1858 they built a town of wooden shacks and fancy sa-
loons where Cherry Creek joined the South Platte River,
and named it Denver, the first permanent settlement in
Colorado.

They chose a dramatic situation for their city. At an
altitude of exactly 5,280 feet, it stands on the western
edge of the great tilted plain that slopes downward and
eastward for a third of a continent to the Mississippi
Valley. Just west of Denver the Rampart Range of the
Rockies rises suddenly out of the flat land like a thou-
sand-mile-long breaker of tossing rock, forever frozen
at the instant it was about to crash down on the sandy
plains.

By 1906 Denver was a city of the second generation,
self-consciously staid and proper on the surface, but still
surging with youthful vitality; the center to which miners
and cattlemen came to spend the wealth they dug out of
the ore-packed mountains or raised on their 10,000-acre
ranches in the plains.

Like all the children of the pioneers, to whom books
were more precious, because rarer, than gold, Denverites
were all out for education, avid for culture. Their public schools were the finest that money and unsparing effort could provide, and because they were certain of a
sellout, all the great actors, musicians, and lecturers of
the era came to enlighten Denver.

Mamie was scarcely conscious of the ebullient life
around Brown's Palace Hotel and up the primrose path
of Market Street. Hers was the small-town Denver,
where the second generation lived on those shady streets
in their ugly, comfortable houses with big grassy back
yards. But even here the western wind swept post-Vic-
torian stuffiness out of the window. Try as they might to

emulate the stodginess of their cultural Mecca, Boston, the people of Denver just could not help being natural and hearty. And, though they aped the East in their cultural pattern, they were enormously proud of their rugged fathers and grandfathers, so that the creed they lived by was a stimulating mixture of Boston Brahminism and the nostalgic memory of gun play on Market Street.

Since Lafayette Street was recently built up there had been no time for cliques to form among the children, so the four Doud girls quickly made friends with all the youngsters of the neighborhood. There were some of every age, and they soon formed the habit of meeting at the hospitable house in mid-block. The front stoop was crowded with little girls sewing dolls clothes. It was then that Mrs. Doud ordered the first red carpet—they have worn out four—spread upon the steps.

Small boys came flocking when Mr. Doud produced a clothes basket full of fireworks on the Fourth of July and filled the evening sky with fiery golden snakes and splendid showers of colored stars, while the whole street rocked with earsplitting reports. He also had a flagpole with a big American flag. It flies now when the President is there.

Mamie's special friends among the girls were Phyllis Eaves and pretty Eileen Ewing, whose parents, Judge and Mrs. Ewing, lived in a big white stucco house on the corner of Seventh Avenue. The whole block was their playground where, with other children of all ages, they played Run Sheep Run or Kick the Can up and down the almost carless streets. Sometimes they turned motherly and pushed their "babies" along the sidewalks in their doll carriages.

Dressing up was Mamie's favorite game. Mrs. Ewing was very clever at making wonderful cartwheel hats ornamented with roses out of crepe paper. Dressed as for a garden party at Buckingham Palace, in their

A. G.

mothers' dresses of lace and silk with trailing skirts and the enormous paper hats, the three little girls, led by Mamie, sashayed around the block, inviting the admiration of the neighborhood.

When the game was over, Mamie could not bear to take off her finery. She would run up to her room and stare admiringly at herself in the mirror, longing for the day when she would really be grown up.

As for the boys, they all adored Mamie, and she re-

ciprocated *in toto*. When they played in the back yard,
the place beside Mamie in the swing was definitely the
seat of honor. As Eileen Ewing, now Mrs. Robert F.
Archibold, says, "When the rest of us were still getting
kicked in the shins by our chivalrous boy friends, Mamie was treated like a Southern belle. One boy cere-
moniously presented her with a genuine rattlesnake skin.
True love could pay no greater tribute."

That first summer in Denver flashed by for Mamie.
Before she knew it, the time had come to go to school
again. Though she did not realize it at the time, Mamie
had the good fortune to go to the best one of all in that
city of fine public schools.

Corona School—now called Dora M. Moore after its
first principal—stood between Eighth and Ninth avenues
on Corona Street. In 1906 Miss Moore was still ruling
it despotically from her small office on the second floor.
She was a little lady, who looked the very archetype of
the spinster schoolmarm in her voluminous black skirts
and white shirtwaists with high boned collars. Her brown
hair was piled in a high pompadour above her small
acquiline face. To complete the picture, she wore pince-
nez on a broad black ribbon.

But it would have been a mistake to take "Biddy"
Moore, as the irreverent called her, at face value. A dynamic spirit inhabited her small body, and she had the
pure passion of a really great teacher for imparting
knowledge. By force of character she broke the Colorado
precedent that executive posts must be held by men, and
became one of the first women principals in the state.
Then she made her school one of the outstanding educa-
tional institutions of its class in the Mountain States.

Even before Mamie went there, Corona had had some

famous graduates. One of them was Douglas Fairbanks, and another was Paul Whiteman. Although both shone in the field of entertainment, never were two small boys more different. Fairbanks was quick and clever both as a student and an athlete. He was a vibrant blade of a boy. Paul Whiteman, according to one aged but forthright teacher, was "a lummox." He never passed a grade and frequently went to sleep in class. When he was awake, his conduct made Mr. Peck's malevolent son seem angelic by comparison. Yet it is impossible to say whether the good boy or the bad contributed more enjoyment to his fellow countrymen and, indeed, to most of the world. Which leaves their tale without a moral.

In addition to its national celebrities, Corona seems to have educated half the eminent lawyers, judges, and educators in Colorado. So great was its reputation that it literally made the section of the city in which it stood the most fashionable part of Denver, for many people moved into the school district just so their children could go to Corona.

The Douds had not heard of its virtues when they moved to Lafayette Street, so it was pure luck that Mamie enjoyed its advantages. How lucky it was may be judged from the fact that it was the only school she ever attended for more than one year.

Though Corona was only a block and a half from the Doud's new home, Eleanor was not allowed to walk even that far. So Mr. Doud sent for Kate. Uncle Joel Carlson brought her out on the train, making frequent trips between his pullman and the baggage car, where Kate occupied a temporary stall, to make sure she was happy and comfortable. Mr. Doud bought a smart little runabout—an open trap with one seat and big wheels picked out in red—in which Eleanor drove to school every morning. Naturally, Mamie and Buster went with her, and kids all along the block piled aboard.

At school Kate was hitched to a tree near the entrance to wait even more patiently than Mary's little lamb for Eleanor to appear. Indeed, she became such a fixture there that her picture later appeared on the covers of the school writing tablets.

To Mamie's eyes her new schoolhouse looked enormous—one of the biggest buildings she had ever seen. It squatted massively on its street corner, with all the ponderous embellishments of nineteenth-century scholastic architecture. Built of red brick, it was irregularly octagon in plan. On four of its eight sides stood beehive-shaped towers capped by strange red cones. The arched doorways were decorated with elaborately carved stonework. Many windows of varied shapes and sizes pierced its walls, and the architect had not missed a single opportunity to add cornices, curlicues, and other jimcrackery. It might have been made of the Anchor blocks with which Buster and Mike played at home.

Mamie was swept up the shallow steps with a crowd of arriving pupils to find herself in a huge, dark, echoing hall that went right up to the lofty roof. Broad stairways sprang from its center to meet on a big landing and branch backward and upward to the second and third floors. Actually, they were very efficiently designed for handling the class-bell rush of hundreds of children racing in opposite directions to different levels. But, to Mamie, they looked like a maze in a cave.

Around the hall were replicas of Greek statues, and on its walls and those of Mamie's classroom hung big plaster models of such classic art as the Parthenon frieze. These were interspersed with steel engravings of famous paintings and portraits of American statesmen. They represented Miss Moore's desperate effort to inculcate her own genuine appreciation of art in her pupils. Since they were hung far above the eye level of a ten-year-old, they signally failed to impress Mamie. The truth of the matter is that, as presented to the pupils of Corona, they were not only dull but downright ugly.

Mamie's classroom, however, was sunnily cheerful, and her teachers were pretty, intelligent young women, the cream of Denver's crop. She loved the school from the first. Not that she studied very hard, or earned terrific marks. The pattern of her scholastic life, established in Cedar Rapids, was repeated. But she was so willing, so gay, and so charming that everyone, including Miss Moore, loved her.

6

To San Antone

THE NEXT SIX YEARS WERE PERHAPS THE HAPPIEST THE
Douds ever knew as a united family. Of course, so
young and energetic a man as Mr. Doud was not content
in retirement. Once his family was well settled in Denver, he again went into harness, which chafes such as he
only when it is removed. However, he arranged his affairs so that he was able to spend much of his time at
home.

They established a very pleasant pattern of life.
Though neither Mr. nor Mrs. Doud cared for society in
the sense of the larger swirl, they made many close
friends among their neighbors, who welcomed them
warmly to Lafayette Street. However, their greatest fun
was doing things as a family.

There was plenty to do. For one thing, Denver was al-

ready the theatrical center of the West, and all the Douds
loved the theater. Almost every Saturday afternoon in
winter Mr. Doud had a box at either the Orpheum or
Pantages Theater. They saw such stars as Sir Harry
Lauder, Blanche Yurka, William Gillette as the immor-
tal Holmes of Baker Street, Edward H. Southern and his
beautiful wife, Julia Marlowe, and lovely young Maude
Adams.

Perhaps the most thrilling performance of all was
Sarah Bernhardt on her farewell tour in *L'Aiglon.* Despite Bernhardt's towering reputation, Mamie was prepared to be bored. How could an old woman possibly
portray a princely youth scarcely eighteen years old?

Mamie's doubts seemed justified for a scene or two
until, without knowing what was happening, she ex-
perienced the miracle of great theater. Gradually the
cracked and painted face of age transformed itself into
the delicate features of a boy, wracked by tragic loyalty
to his imperial father. The almost comically obese figure in the tight breeches of a French cavalry officer
mysteriously changed into the emaciated form of the
heir to the throne of France, wasting away in the palace
of his enemies. Bernhardt actually *became* the proud
Eaglet who would not bend to fate.

As he died in the arms of his last loyal aide, Mamie
was convulsed by heartbroken sobs. She refused to be
comforted until the Douds made their usual stop at
Baur's Confectionery Store where she consumed a
"Teddy Bear," consisting of vanilla ice cream with
chocolate sauce, sprinkled with nuts and topped by a
maraschino cherry.

In summertime all Denver went to Elitch's Gardens,
which is the most famous amusement park in America—

with the possible exception of Coney Island. Mamie was ten years old the first time her father took the family there. They went by trolley car, for the Gardens were far out in the country northwest of the city. Anticipation

heightened with every mile as the open trolley rocked over the badly laid tracks at the exhilarating speed of twenty miles an hour. When at last Mamie passed through the elaborate gatehouse of Elitch's with its intricate wooden latticework and columned arcade, she felt like Dorothy entering the wonderful Land of Oz.

First came a zoo, with bears and all manner of native and imported wildlife. There were camels to ride and an ostrich that pulled a two-wheeled sulky at racing

speed. Drowsing in his cage was old Rex, the lion who
served as a model for the majestic beasts that still guard
the entrance to the Chicago Art Museum.

The strident strains of a steam calliope drew them on
to the merry-go-round, which was housed in a huge circular building with an undulating roof like the tent of
Kublai Khan. All the animals of Noah's Ark, together
with swan boats, palanquins, and a Roman chariot
swirled around three abreast, rising and falling with exciting sweeps. For her first ride Mamie chose the chariot,
on which you stood behind a curving shield and pretended you were driving three galloping horses abreast
like Ben Hur. It remains her favorite vehicle to this day.

Another attraction was the Old Mill, which Mamie
found rather scarey. In fact, she did not fully appreciate
its possibilities until some years later, when, as a young
lady, she came to Elitch's with her beaux. You got into a
long, narrow boat and sailed along a dark and winding
river in perfect blackness until around some corner a
vivid tableau met your enchanted eyes. There in a fairy
glade was Snow White and her dwarfs, with the prince
riding over the hill on his white horse. Another corner
and you were on the African veld with horribly realistic
lions glowering at you from the bushes not six feet away.

After the emotional stresses of Roman chariots and
lions—caged or stuffed—it was nice to have a picnic
lunch on a rustic table in the famous old apple orchard,
which had been the foundation of the original Elitch
ranch.

Elitch's also had a theater and a resident stock company, the oldest in America. Every year Mrs. Elitch
engaged some famous star to head the company. So great
was the prestige of the theater that it is said no actor

ever refused an invitation to play there. In 1908, Mamie saw Belasco's famous star, David Warfield, play his greatest role in *The Music Master*. Warfield was supported by a Denver girl, young Antoinette Perry.

William Collier, Milton Sills, and Louise Woods headed the players in other years, while in a single season (1913) Ralph Morgan, Pedro de Corboda, Jean Selby, and Spring Byington were regular members of the company. Thus Mamie's education in appreciation of the theater was perhaps more complete than if she had lived in dramatically favored New York, where, because of the glut of theatrical riches spread before them, people often do not bother to go.

Another favorite treat was a family expedition to hear the band concert in City Park and watch the fountain play. As Mamie grew older, these weekly expeditions became something of a bore because they interfered with her dates. But Mr. Doud was adamant. Once a custom had been established, he stuck to it; and the whole family had to go along whether they liked it or not.

There were also short trips to the mountains where they spent the night in cabins by pleasantly noisy streams and the air in mid-summer took on an icy edge from the snow-capped peaks to the westward. But however much she enjoyed all these divertisements, the thing Mamie remembers best is the fun they had at home.

The Douds gave parties for the girls at the slightest excuse—on birthdays, of course; Thanksgiving; Hallowe'en, when they combed the countryside for cornstalks and pumpkins to decorate the cellar. They even gave parties on holidays like Washington's Birthday, or for no good reason at all except that they felt like it. Usually they were quite elaborate, with decorations thought up by

Mrs. Doud to suit the occasion. Sometimes they were no more than asking some children over to roast potatoes in burning leaves in the gutter. But whatever the party was, everybody who was asked came—and had a good time.

In September, 1910, the older Douds made a decision that altered the whole course of Mamie's life. Indeed, it is not too farfetched to suppose that history itself might have been different had they elected another course. For Ike and Mamie are what the President often refers to as "a winning team"; and had they never met, he might not have developed as he did.

The immediate reason for the Douds' decision was Eleanor's health. She was now fifteen, a fragile, lovely girl, who to one small, bookish boy on Lafayette Street seemed the personification of the Lady of Shalott. Her physical languor did not slow her brain. She was avid for knowledge and easily the most brilliant member of the family.

Eleanor was not improving. To the anxious eyes of her father and mother she seemed, indeed, to be very gradually drifting away. This was especially true during the short but frigid Denver winters. Her doctors thought that a season in some warm and sunny climate might turn the tide.

There was no doubt in the minds of Mr. and Mrs. Doud about following this advice. The only question was where to go. Florida was then a faraway, elongated sand bar inhabited by Seminole Indians, clam diggers, and a few flamboyant millionaires; southern California with its torrential rainy season seemed unappealing. They settled on San Antonio in the warm southern part of Texas.

It was a gay safari. They drove down in their splendid

new Winton Six. Landers and Dawson, their two Negro menservants, rode in front, alternating at the wheel. Mr. and Mrs. Doud and the four little girls, begoggled and muffled to the ears in dusters and veils, filled the ample tonneau. They steered by the *Blue Book* over the dusty, high-crowned roads across the empty desert; down through the hamlet of Amarillo; through Fort Worth, still a cow town; past Waxahachie. . . . On fine days Landers and Dawson put the unwieldy top down. Showers or evening chill, and up it went again. Top up, top down, all the way.

As they drove along, they all sang songs, wished on a load of hay. The girls played an intricate numbers game with the licenses of the few cars they met. Usually, Eleanor won.

In the evening they stopped at a hotel. The girls dressed up in their best silk dresses for dinner. Mamie brushed the dust out of her long hair and wore it down her back with a big bow of red ribbon fastened by a gold barrette. After dinner they all walked around the town in the soft Southern air.

The Douds liked San Antonio almost as well as Denver—so well that they bought a house there. It was bigger than the Denver house, made of white clapboards, with tall white columns in front. Mrs. Doud called it "very snarky." This house assured their eventual return.

As they drove back to Denver, young Ike Eisenhower was rolling eastward in a day coach on his way to West Point.

7

The Last of School

THE DOUDS DID NOT GO BACK TO SAN ANTONIO THE FOL-
lowing winter for a most melancholy reason. Eleanor
was failing rapidly, and was too ill to travel. Early in
1912 her courageous little heart gave up the fight.

Eleanor's death was a great blow to all the people of
the neighborhood. Years later, one of them said, "I
never saw people sorrow so for one not their own."

Because of her brilliant mind, Eleanor could talk on
an equal level with her parents' friends and seemed to
enjoy being with them as much as with the young people,
who adored her. The little boys like Edward Bird and
John Askling, who often came to sit beside her as she re-
clined on the Douds' front porch, were stricken with the
brief but piercing sorrow of childhood.

Eleanor's funeral service at the Corona Street Presbyterian Church, where the Douds worshiped and the children went to Sunday School, was crowded far beyond the capacity of the small building. There was no person there who did not feel an intimate sense of loss.

Poignant though their grief, and wide though the gap that Eleanor left in the family circle, the Douds were too strong and sensible to be shattered by sorrow. They closed ranks and went on with their life. Nor would they permit Eleanor's passing to shadow the lives of their other daughters for long.

The girls were all growing up. The time had come when Buster and Mike must put off their boys' clothes and wear dresses, though they still kept their short Dutch-boy hair cuts with straight bangs across their foreheads. Blue-eyed Buster loved her pretty new dresses, but Mike was irreconcilable. The day Mrs. Doud first made her wear a dress, she sat screaming in the vegetable garden in the back yard. Whenever anyone approached her, she hurled cucumbers at them with deadly accuracy.

That June Mamie was graduated from Corona School. Since there were no junior high schools in those days and many boys and girls did not go beyond the eighth grade, much more to-do was made about graduating from grade school than is customary now. Corona gave her graduates the full treatment—presentation of awards, speeches, and songs.

Miss Jessie Hamilton, who was Mamie's eighth-grade teacher, always tried to impress on her pupils that the records they left behind them, even in the grades, followed them through life. In Mamie's case this is to her advantage, for despite her lack of studious application she was highly regarded by her teachers. Speaking of her dependability Miss Hamilton said, "If you wanted a job well done, you gave it to Mamie!"

Dressed in traditional white organdie, with her long hair down her back, caught by a big white bow, Mamie made her contribution to the graduation exercises by singing in her lovely, though untrained, voice "Where the Four-leaf Clover Grows."

However, this was not Mamie's first public appearance. Three years before, when she was only twelve years old, she had been asked to sing before the Denver Women's Club.

Though she studied piano all through her girlhood and played with a fine sense of rhythm and shading, Mamie never had a voice lesson in her life. The Carlsons were all musically inclined, and her ability to sing true and sweet was a natural gift. It was infinitely appealing when combined with her warm and vivid personality, which came right across the footlights and embraced her audience.

At the Women's Club she sang in costume, a Kelly-green skirt and a black velvet bodice laced with green ribbon over a white blouse. She wore black patent-leather pumps, green socks, and a big green bow in her hair. Under the lights her dark blue eyes shone like living jewels, and the flush of excitement in the transparency of her skin was far more vivid than rouge.

Her first song was "Believe Me if All Those Endearing Young Charms." At the thunder of applause, led, of course, by Mrs. Doud and Mamie's three sisters, she came out again. This time Mamie was carrying a little white plaster-of-Paris pig. A green saddle, which Mrs. Doud had made with infinite care, hid the advertising slogan printed on the pig by its makers, Swift's Meat Packing Company.

For her encore Mamie sang:

> As I was walking down the street
>   from Tipperary Town,
> I met a little colleen with lovely
>   eyes of brown.
> I said, 'Perhaps you're married,'
> She said, 'Perhaps I'm not. . . .
> The little pigs had done it.
> Och! the dear little girl.

The whole thing was a resounding success. But whatever Mamie may have dreamed in that first flush of audience acclaim, there is no indication that she ever was the least bit stage struck.

Despite their fondness for Denver, the Douds were great travelers. One year they took Mamie and Buster down to Panama, sailing from New Orleans in a United Fruit ship. There Mamie savored for the first time the strangeness of extravagant tropical scenes and thick, sweet tropical smells, which were to become as familiar to her as the hard, clean atmosphere of Denver. She sailed up the broad aqueous steps of Balboa Locks and along that thin, metallic-looking ribbon of water, which had just joined two great oceans with the cord of commerce. As the ship passed through the man-made fjord of the Culebra Cut and on to the gentler slopes near the Pacific, she might have seen, if she looked up, the delapidated French villa that would be one of her many transient homes.

Another trip took the Douds and Uncle Joel Carlson

by steamer through the Great Lakes, then to Albany via Lake George and down the Hudson. Their boat was one of the splendid white and gold sidewheelers that skedaddled at delicious speed down the river between the green, rounded domes of the Catskills—so different from the jagged, snow-capped peaks of the Rockies— and the gentle slopes of the east bank. Uncle Joel, who was a gay and knowledgeable bachelor, pointed out some of the historic places to Mamie. There was Clermont, a graceful white house on a low cliff, behind which terraced lawns rose to a dark wall of trees. Joel said the Livingstons had lived there for nearly 200 years, and Robert Fulton, who had married a daughter of the house, named the first steamboat after it. Then came Frederic Vanderbilt's huge granite "cottage" with the high corinthian columns and massive façade so typical of the Age of Ostentation. They completely missed a pleasant Victorian frame house, nestling among tall trees a little farther down the river—nobody ever had heard of Hyde Park.

Below Poughkeepsie the river narrowed to a thread between lowering mountains that cut off the sun and sent a chill down Mamie's back. Uncle Joel pointed to a plateau jutting out into the stream on which stood fortresslike buildings with crenelated towers. "That's West Point," he said. "How would you like to be up there dancing with all those handsome kaydets?"

Mamie gave him her broad grin and answered, "I'd love it."

In New York Mamie saw all the sights from the new Woolworth Building to Coney Island, which was nearly as much fun as Elitch's. Most of the theaters were closed for the summer, but they saw *The Pink Lady*, a "terrific" musical comedy.

The Douds came home by way of Quebec and up the Saint Lawrence through the Thousand Islands. At Owen Sound on Lake Huron, they ran into a colossal storm. the peculiarly vicious, short-length waves of the Great Lakes smashed against the little steamer, sending icy spray flying over the bridge. Mr. and Mrs. Doud lay groaning in their cabin, and even Uncle Joel's face wore the olive-drab signs of a queasy stomach; but Mamie felt fine. She spent her time in the wheelhouse watching the bow point skyward, then plunge under tons of churning green and white water. The captain told her, as captains always will, "In forty years, man and boy on the Lakes, this is the worst storm I ever seen."

Back in Denver Mamie played the sophisticated traveler for her friends. Then she had a most embarrassing experience. She was allowed to go dancing with her uncle at the Trocadero at Elitch's, because the place was very strictly run. No alcoholic drinks were served, not even beer.

Joel, with the Carlson sense of rhythm in his toes, was a splendid dancer, and they whirled madly in waltzes and two-steps. Finally the band played a syncopated rhythm.

"Let's see if we can do that new Turkey Trot we saw in New York," Mamie said.

"Sure we can," said Uncle Joel.

Hesitantly at first, and then with joyous abandon, they footed it, clutched in the curiously clumsy embrace that the dance required. Came a dreadful tap on Uncle Joel's shoulder. His face turned purple, and Mamie blushed right down to her heels.

The uniformed attendant was saying, "The management requests that you dance a little less spectacularly."

Mamie's formal education continued sporadically. She went for a short time to the East Denver High School. In San Antonio she attended the Mulholland School, which was later merged with St. Mary's Hall. The three girls went to Mrs. Hayden's dancing school in Denver. Each Saturday morning they started out by streetcar in their pretty silk party frocks, carrying their dancing slippers.

There Mamie had her first date when she was sixteen. It was for an evening dance at Mrs. Hayden's, and she well remembers the dress she wore—pink silk, with puffed sleeves and a long full skirt. It had an extremely modest round neckline. Her date's name was Jimmy Cassell. Thus he gains a brief flash of immortality and disappears from history.

Mamie's one full year of high school was at Miss Wolcott's "finishing school." This institution was the most fashionable in Denver—"very katish," they called it. It had remarkable facilities for that era—a large auditorium with a stage and an elaborate organ, a studio where fine arts were taught, a gymnasium, a swimming pool, and even a bowling alley!

Miss Anna Wolcott, sister of Colorado's Senator Edward Wolcott, founded it and ran it as a rather interesting combination of an old-style academy for young ladies of refinement and a modern, progressive school where intelligence was actually fostered by brilliant teachers and athletics were emphasized. *"Mens sana in corpore sano,"* Miss Wolcott would have said.

The founder's personal philosophy was expressed in the verses painted on the wall of the auditorium:

> One ship drives East
> Another West
> While the selfsame breezes blow.
> It's the set of the sails
> And not the gales
> That bids them where to go.

The second verse stated that people were like ships in-as much as:

> The set of the soul
> Determines the goal.

The school motto was *Noblesse Oblige*.

Mamie's fellow pupils at Miss Wolcott's found her shy and quiet. Somehow her natural ebullience never seemed to break out in school. She was conscientious but uninspired. Professor Quarles, striving to drive Euclid's propositions into her head, suspected that she was smart, but he could not prove it.

Athletics, practiced in the great baggy bloomers that modesty required before the great emancipation of women's legs, left Mamie as cold as a fish on ice. Her one accomplishment in this field was ice skating, which she performed with all the grace and rhythm that made her such a superb dancer.

However, the year at Miss Wolcott's was far from wasted. She won the close friendship of many of her schoolmates and acquired social poise without chilling her natural warmth, a combination of assets invaluable to a hostess.

The great event of the year at Miss Wolcott's was

8

Now That She Was a Young Lady

THE WINTER OF 1914-15 WAS THE LAST YEAR MAMIE went to school. She was eighteen years old. Now that she was a young lady, Mr. Doud took her education in hand and taught her some things that were extremely important in her later career.

The relationship between father and daughter was very close and affectionate. He often called her "Puddin'," after Puddin' Head Wilson, and she nicknamed him "Pooh Bah," from the character in *The Mikado* who likes to run everything. They joked with each other constantly, yet now Mr. Doud would be considered a very strict father; his word was the law of his house.

Indeed, to one of Mamie's younger beaux he seemed "gigantic and forbidding."

Under his careful tutelage, Mamie learned to keep accounts of everything she spent. She had an adequate allowance, and she had to live within it. If she ran out of money it was just too bad. However, if a real crisis arose, "Poppa was quick with the checkbook."

Mamie learned to run a house from her mother, who was considered one of the most efficient housekeepers in Denver. The Douds had quite an establishment with five in the family, four servants, and innumerable guests. Buying food for so many and utilizing it so there was no waste was good practice. Mamie learned how to select cuts of meat and what to pay for them. Twenty-five cents a pound was the maximum price you should pay for porterhouse steak—that was one lesson she soon had to unlearn.

So Mamie's father trained her in the careful management of money that enabled her to live comfortably on an Army officer's pay. It was well he did, for Ike had no interest in money matters. From the first he handed Mamie the purse strings. Indeed, years later Eisenhower told his son John that if the latter did not drink or smoke until he was twenty-one he would receive $300. Then Ike had a second thought: "Say, Mamie, have we got three hundred dollars?"

As for running a large establishment, it was many years before Mamie had a chance to practice what her mother had taught her. But when the time arrived, her knowledge surely came in handy.

There was one gaping void in Mamie's home-taught domestic-science course. She hated cooking and would not learn how. It remained for her husband to teach her.

Though love made her a willing pupil, Ike is still the better cook because he practices the art with loving care.

Nineteen-fifteen was Mamie's last summer in Denver, though of course nobody knew that. The happy pattern of home was so well established that it seemed as though it would go on forever. When the Douds were all alone, there was a pool game or music in the evening. The expeditions to the theater and the band concerts were as fixed events as the transit of Venus. Parties followed the inevitable course of birthdays and holidays; and every Sunday evening the Douds held open house for any of their friends who wanted to drop in for buffet supper, served as a sort of smörgasbord.

Kate had been replaced by the famous electric. When the day came for her to retire to a farm and give her stall in the Douds' small garage on Corona Street to the new machine, all three girls burst into tears.

That summer Mamie learned to drive Creepy. One of

the sights of Denver was Mamie in a party dress and a big picture hat making a stately progress through the streets in the gleaming splendor of the beautiful little car. However, she was seldom alone, for all the small boys of the neighborhood wanted a ride, and she could not resist them.

Sometimes it seemed that she could never be alone at all; for her beaux constantly importuned her for dates or simply came to call. Usually they arrived in groups to sit on the red carpet and sing or talk, eating and drinking enormous quantities of cookies and grape juice. They were all ages and sorts, from shy George Sibley who would run across the street with a huge box of candy, place his present on the doormat, ring the bell and run away in a panic; to Vance McMannus, who was an older man of twenty-five with a job in the bank daytimes and in the band at night. He often brought his quartet to serenade Mamie. One New Year's Day Vance and a dozen of his friends had hired a city water wagon on which to pay their New Year's calls. They arrived at Lafayette Street with Vance driving the two draft horses. All over the fat barrel of the cart, astride the team, and even perched on the sprayers, were young men formally dressed in black broadcloth suits and derby hats.

Mamie went out more than all the rest of the Douds combined. Groups of young people overflowing big, dilapidated touring cars would drive up and sound their musical bugle horns. Mamie would hastily stick a beauty spot just below her left cheekbone and dash out in a flutter of long skirts, holding her black picture hat on with one hand and carrying her white gloves in the other; and off they would go to a ten-cent movie downtown or to dance at Elitch's, where you got one dance and two choruses for a nickel.

The young men generally belonged to social clubs with peculiar names like the Siama Diama Club. These were mostly for the purpose of giving parties; sometimes, little dinner dances; sometimes, picnics in the hills. At the picnics the men often came dressed in regular business suits with straw hats, but they did unbend so far as to take their coats off.

A special kind of party that they all loved was to hire an open trolley car, and go careening off to Golden or some other remote town. Most fun of all was the ride back through the summer night with the stars so close that you could reach out and grab them if you were not too busy holding your beau's hand. One night the trolley broke down, and Mamie did not get home until the depraved hour of 3:00 A.M. Pooh Bah was not pleased.

As the fall drew near, there were many melancholy young men in Denver. Mamie was going to San Antonio for the winter, and spring seemed an ice age away. She comforted them as much as she could, and promised them she would write, and that she would soon be coming home.

Just as the Douds were piling into the new Packard twin-six, a delegation of the faithful arrived to see Mamie off. There were Jack Phelps and Dudley Mayo; Tom Ryan, Russell Writer, George Sibley from across the street, and Vance McMannus, who had taken a few hours off from the Colorado National Bank. Mamie leaned out of the car to give them each her hand and promised again to come back soon.

"Supposing you fall in love with some guy in San Antone?" asked Vance, his round red face looking unaccustomedly sad.

"I won't do that," said Mamie gaily. "There's nobody in Texas that I specially like."

9

Mamie Walks Post

THE DOUDS MOTORED SOUTHWARD, FOLLOWING THE routine they had established. No need to look in the *Blue Book* now; they knew the short cuts and the best hotels all along the familiar way. On a train that would beat them to San Antonio by a couple of days were Mrs. Doud's electric, and the two maids, who would have the house ready for them. Their customary hegira was as well organized as a perfectly executed military maneuver—far better, in fact, than some logistics that were taking place simultaneously.

It was raining in Galveston. Tropical downpours on sun-baked earth too hard to absorb water resulted in a spectacular run-off that flooded low-lying sections of the city. In the barracks of the Nineteenth Infantry the water rose steadily. When it reached the level of an Army cot, the colonel wired Washington and received orders transferring his command to Fort Sam Houston at San Antonio. He could not get out quick enough to please himself and his men. Carrying their equipment on their heads, they waded through thigh-deep water to the waiting trains.

A second lieutenant just out of West Point, arriving to report for his first tour of duty, found the camp deserted. Cussing his luck and the ways of the Army, he bought a ticket for San Antonio.

The first Sunday in October was a beautiful sunny day, warmer than Denver in mid-summer. But Mamie was not too pleased when Mr. Doud said, "The Ingrums are taking us for a drive this afternoon. I'd like you to come with us."

"Oh Pooh Bah, I've got a date at seven. We may not get back in time."

"Certainly we will," her father said. "Come along."

There was not anything else to do, so she agreed.

In the Ingrums' touring car they drove through the narrow, winding streets of the city, which seemed more Latin than American, so strong was the impress of its founders. Mexican families in their chromatic Sunday best sat on doorsteps or strolled in the little parks.

When they got out of town to the tawny countryside, Judge Ingrum suggested they visit the Harrises at Fort Sam.

"I've got to be home at seven," Mamie warned him.

"That will be easy," he answered. "We'll just drop by for a short call."

Major Harris and the Misses Addabel and Lulu Harris were sitting in deck chairs on the sparkling green lawn between their red brick Army house and the long,

galleried Bachelor Officers' Quarters. There was a whirl
of greetings, and they all sat down while Miss Lulu went
to fetch a pitcher of the inevitable grape juice. It was not
long before the honey displayed at the threshold of the
hive lured the bees out of the B.O.Q. Two young officers
strolled negligently across the turf. Mamie recognized
Lieutenants James Byrom and Leonard Gerow. She was
glad she had worn her starched white linen dress and the
big, floppy black hat, which she knew very well made her
look charmingly ethereal. The young officers reacted
properly, and Mamie began to sparkle. "Tell me the
news of the Fort," she said.

Lieutenants Byrom and Gerow began to cut their own
throats.

"We've got a new shavetail," said Byrom. "Football
star till he busted his knee."

"He's a real good guy," said Gerow. "Handsome,
too."

"Oh, I don't know about that," Byrom objected. "Sure
he's nice looking, but handsome?"

"Of course he's handsome," said Miss Lulu.

"Bring out your paragon and let me judge," laughed
Mamie.

Gerow obediently swung around and bellowed at the
B.O.Q., "Hey Ike!"

"Be right over," was the resonant reply.

He came across the sunlit stretch of turf, walking with
the measured stride of his cadet training, yet somehow
casually. Mamie could see that he was fresh out of the
Point, with the shine and polish still on him. His boots
were mahogany mirrors; his brass buttons glittered like
trinkets in a jeweler's window, and his khaki uniform
was poured to the mold of his stalwart figure. Because

he was Officer of the Guard that day, he wore a service revolver in the holster of his broad belt.

"He's a bruiser," she thought admiringly, looking at his hard, broad shoulders, and round, ruddy face. His eyes were blue and twinkly. As he drew near, he took off his cap and the sunlight splashed on his yellow hair. He grinned at them, not nervously, but with disarming friendliness. Even before she was introduced, Mamie felt as though she knew him well.

"Miss Doud," said Miss Lulu formally, "may I present Mr. Eisenhower?"

"Of course you may," said Mamie.

Then he was bowing in the stiff cadet way, holding her hand with gentle strength, and looking at her as though he were trying to memorize her face for always. For just a moment his eyes were intensely blue and serious. Then they crinkled again with laughter as he said, "Miss Doud, it really is a pleasure."

Mamie laughed as though that were a Wildean witticism. Then she realized it was not that funny, blushed a little, and wondered why she suddenly felt so gay. Ike was laughing too. At nothing in particular.

The afternoon raced away, until Judge Ingrum mindful of Mamie's instructions, looked at his watch and said, "It's time to be getting back."

"Is it really? Oh dear," Mamie sighed.

"Why don't you stay for supper at the Officers' Mess?" Miss Lulu asked.

"That's a wonderful idea," Ike seconded.

"I'm really sorry, but I have a date," Mamie said.

"Put him off," suggested Miss Lulu, the matchmaker.

"I can't do that," Mamie objected. "But perhaps I could phone and tell him to call for me here."

So it was arranged. The older Douds and the Ingrums left. Judge Ingrum was in a state of some bemusement, but Mr. Doud, with more experience of his daughter, saw how the wind blew and was not surprised.

It was a merry party in the big bare room of the mess. Laughter echoed off the high ceiling, while less fortunate officers stared in envy. Both Ike and Mamie were in tremendous spirits, setting the pace of gaiety.

When the meal was over, Ike rose regretfully. "I've got to inspect the guard," he said. "Would you like to walk post with me, Miss Mamie?"

Mamie was not especially fond of walking, and she had seen all of Fort Sam she ever wanted to see. She could not have been more surprised when she heard herself say, "I'd love to."

They walked together through the soft, golden evening, talking with easy companionship. Of course, there were numerous interruptions. Ike's hand was forever snapping up to the visor of his cap in correct acknowledgment of the salutes of passing enlisted men. At every post Mamie stood aside while the guard turned out, and Ike inspected each piece of equipment with the meticulous attention of every young officer on his first tour of duty.

So they progressed through the long, straight avenues of the Fort, lined with the white-trimmed, red brick buildings that make all Army posts look the same, from Fort Devon, Massachusetts, to Manila. As they passed a long barracks, Ike said delicately, "Don't look up. The boys aren't too careful about pulling down the shades."

Without meaning to, Mamie instinctively stared up at rows of open windows. Ike's laughter ricocheted down the quiet street. "If that isn't just like a woman!"

Post Number Five was the last but one, and then the Hospital Post. Inspection over, Mamie sat down beside Ike on the broad wooden steps of Brooke Hospital to rest and talk some more.

Although Mamie always remembered the details of that day with complete clarity—even what people said— she was never quite sure what she and Ike talked about as they sat and watched the sunset spread the spectrum across the Texas sky. All she recalled was the wonderful sense of ease. This big, genial young man was not like any other beau she had ever had—already she knew he was a beau. There were no pretty compliments, none of the playful fencing of early courtship at which she was so adept. Instead they talked sensibly about all sorts of things besides themselves. Yet they got to know each other very quickly.

This Ike was a restful fellow to be with; and, contradictorily, stimulating, too. Mamie found that she was talking better than she thought she could. Ike drew out the best in one, without effort or strain. That was the part of being with him that she liked best, the complete absence of tension. He was so simple and direct, so unpretending, that she could relax and take it easy, just as he did.

In fact, Mamie relaxed so completely that her date had an outrageously long wait.

The next day she went fishing at Medina Lake. It is a sport that encourages cerebration; Mamie had time to think a good deal about Mr. Eisenhower. She wondered when he would call—not if, just when.

Lucius, the Douds' new butler, had the answer when she came home. "Miss Mamie, a Mr. Eisenhart's been calling you, an' ef he's phoned once he's phoned fifteen times!"

Mamie giggled. "You must mean Mr. Eisenhower."

"Yes, Miss, Mr. Eisenhart. Lordy! There he goes again!"

Although Ike spoke with formal politeness he sounded confident. "Miss Mamie, will you give me the pleasure of going dancing with me tonight?"

Mamie's mental reaction was, "Does he really think he can date me on two hours' notice?" But she put sweet regret into her voice as she told Ike she had an engagement.

"Tomorrow night then?"

That, too, was impossible.

"How about the dance at the Majestic Saturday night?"

This was ridiculous. Every girl who was anything was dated 'way ahead for the big Saturday nights at the Majestic. This young man had better learn the facts of life.

"I'm sorry, Mr. Eisenhower, but I'm dated for the Majestic for the next three weeks."

"All right, four weeks from Saturday then," said the indefatigable Eisenhower.

"I'd love that," said Mamie.

Having made her point, she regretted it. "I'm usually home about five," she volunteered. "You might call some afternoon."

Said Ike, "I'll be there tomorrow."

Ike was there tomorrow, and many tomorrows. If Mamie was not at home, he talked to the Douds and seemed quite happy. That was a special point for him. Most other young men seemed uneasy in the presence of her parents, forever trying to get her off alone. That made for tension, especial in such a close-knit family group. Ike never maneuvered for seclusion. Indeed, he often talked as much with Mrs. Doud as with Mamie. His attitude would have been high strategy had it been planned, but it was not. There was no trace of Machiavelli in his make-up. He really liked them all.

Equally good was his reaction to the Douds' manner of living. That is, he had no reaction at all; he took them as they came. The big, white, shingled house on McCullough Street, with its wide, curving verandas and tall Corinthian columns, was the finest home this young man from Abilene ever had entered. Lucius, serving tea from the old English silver service, was far beyond Ike's experience. Yet he was not impressed. He paid no heed to this lush living, for he was not interested in such things at all, nor was he conscious of social demarcations. Of all the people who profess to be democratic, he was that rare bird who really is. Not only did he never feel superior to anyone, he never felt *inferior*, which is logical, but difficult for most.

It was only gradually that Mamie learned about Ike's background. He had many things to talk about beside himself. Once started, though, he loved to reminisce about the small white house in Abilene, Kansas, where he was reared; his five rampaging brothers, his gentle, dreamy father, and his intensely vital mother. Mamie soon realized that Ida Eisenhower was the mainspring of that family.

Ike told her that he was born in Denison, Texas, in a small house by the railroad tracks. His father, David Eisenhower, drove an engine for the Cotton Belt Railroad. They had moved to Abilene when Mr. Eisenhower got a job as chief engineer of the Belle Springs Creamery. They had lived there ever since.

The Eisenhowers were of German descent. Their ancestors had left their homeland in the wave of emigration caused by religious persecution in the eighteenth century. They had settled first, and prospered, in Pennsylvania, then moved on to Kansas after the Civil War. They were Brethren in Christ, popularly known as River Brethren, because they believed in baptism in rivers, like John and Jesus in the Jordan. Ike himself did not belong to the sect, for he could not believe in all their tenets, though he had strong faith in God.

When Mamie asked him about the Brethren, Ike told her they were a plain sect something like the Quakers and, like them, believed that to make war was a great sin. His mother, Ida Eisenhower, had an especial hatred of war, because she had been born in Virginia and had seen the armies of the North and South fight through her father's land; had watched men dying in the fields beyond the barnyard fence; had known the horrid smell of wounds.

"Yet she let you become a soldier," Mamie said. "How did that happen?"

"Mother is a most unusual sort of mother," Eisenhower said. "She thinks that if you are raised right, your conscience will tell you what is right for you. She would not interfere with her children's decisions."

"But why did you choose the Army?" Mamie asked.

"We were too poor for me to go to college," Ike answered frankly. "It was the only way I could get an education."

That business of getting an education was vitally important to the Eisenhowers. Ike's father was a graduate of Lane College, Kansas. So was his mother. She had used her small inheritance to achieve a college education, which few women had, or even wanted, then.

So, although David Eisenhower had always been in the lower financial brackets, earning at best $1,800 a year, he had been in the upper realm of learning, familiar with the classics of English literature and the Bible. Like Mr. Doud, the Eisenhowers read to their children almost every evening. Mrs. Eisenhower loved music and often played for them on the small upright piano that was her one extravagance. Ike himself loved to sing, but the first time she heard him, Mamie's ears suffered a sharp twinge. He never learned to keep on key.

These were the only similarities in the upbringing of Mamie and Ike. In other respects their early lives hardly could have been less alike. With so many children and so little money all the Eisenhowers had had to pitch in. Ike had worked hard ever since he was seven years old, when he and his brother Edgar used to drag a toy express wagon full of vegetables they had raised across the tracks to the more prosperous section of Abilene, and peddle them from door to door.

Besides doing his share of the housework and the chores of their two-and-one-half acre farm, young Ike had all sorts of jobs—as a harvest hand, at the Abilene Bottling Company, in garages, paper routes, and sandpapering horses in the merry-go-round factory.

When they were in high school, Ike and Edgar shared the job of night fireman at the Belle Springs Creamery, working alternate nights. When he was on duty, Ike spent the whole night in the cavernous engine room of the creamery. He had a broken-down easy chair right in the middle of the floor between the firedoors of the huge silver boilers and the shining wheels and cylinders of the great stationary engine. A naked electric bulb hung from the ceiling on a long wire. By its light he did his homework. Later he caught cat naps. Every hour he had to wake and tend the fires. In those days he never got enough sleep.

When he finished high school, Ike became night superintendent of the creamery, and held part-time day jobs as well. He earned a good deal of money, most of which he sent to Edgar to help him through college. In addition he learned to play a cracking good game of poker in the permanent poker game in the basement of Joner Callahan's drugstore.

That way a year went by. Ike knew he was drifting. It was then he decided he had to have more education. Since it took all the Eisenhowers' spare cash to keep Edgar in college, Ike had to get it free. The only way was at one of the service schools, Annapolis or West Point. Ike went back to high school and boned up, after which he took competitive examinations for both Army and Navy. He won the Navy one, which was his choice. Then he found that, at twenty, he was too old to enter the naval academy. Meanwhile he had placed second in the Army examination. The boy who won failed his physical examination, and Eisenhower got the appointment.

When Ike was graduated from the military academy, he chose the infantry and applied for service in the Philippines. He was told he could have it, and he bought a full set of tropical uniforms. Instead, he was ordered to join the Nineteenth Infantry Regiment at Galveston, and got there after they had left. Such was his round-about route from Denison to San Antonio.

10

To Marry an Army Man?

IKE'S DECISION HAD BEEN IMPETUOUS; THAT FIRST DAY
at Fort Sam he knew Mamie was the girl for him. Love
at first sight is banal to say, but a unique miracle when
it happens to you. However, his courtship was not hasty.
In military terms it was not a full-dress attack, but
rather a matter of persistent pressure and infiltration.
Almost imperceptibly he became a member of the family.

At first Mamie did not realize what was happening.
There was the matter of those football games at Peacock
Academy. As soon as he arrived at Fort Sam, preceded
by his West Point reputation, Ike was asked to coach the
Peacock eleven. It was a good high school team, and he
made it a superior one by throwing himself into the job
with as much ardor as though he were coaching the
cadets to meet the midshipmen. Ike's enthusiasms were

as contagious as measles. All the Douds caught fire from him. They went to every game that Peacock played, and cheered themselves hoarse.

Mamie had never been a sports enthusiast; she could not have cared less if the Red Sox beat the Phillies in the World Series, and she was completely indifferent to the fortunes of the University of Colorado's football team. But suddenly she found that it mattered terribly whether or not Peacock triumphed over West Texas Military Academy.

She sat in the roofless wooden grandstand on a somber November day, with a cold rain trickling unheeded down her neck, her hair streaming in untidy whisps as a Texas Norther whipped it. Her smart velvet hat was a sodden wreck; her voice, a croak except when it rose to a shrill scream as Peacock scored. Had she stopped to think about herself she would have been horrified by her appearance, though blue eyes, brilliant with excitement, and flushed, rain-wet cheeks were hardly unbecoming. But she forgot about herself as she triumphantly cheered Peacock—cheered "Ike's boys" to victory.

Mamie told herself it was because Peacock was such a game little school.

Things began to get serious around Christmas time. To Ike, who never had had any money at all, a second lieutenant's pay—less than $150 a month—was riches. By habit he was frugal with himself, but nothing he could afford was too fine for Mamie and her family. On her nineteenth birthday, November 14, Ike was asked to the family dinner, so far had he moved in a month. He arrived with the biggest box of candy he could find. At Christmas he really outdid himself. Mrs. Doud, Buster, and Mike each got a fine silver compact on a chain.

For Mamie there was a heart-shaped, silver jewel case,
beautifully wrought. It was so handsome that it looks
appropriate on Mamie's dressing table in the White
House.

So far Mamie had been drifting happily on the rising
tide of her affection for Ike. Meanwhile her other beaux,
seeing what everyone but Mamie saw, began to slide
away. They had a few disgruntled remarks to make to
the effect that "brass buttons always get them," and a
pointed reminder that San Antonio was known as "the
mother-in-law of the Army," because so many girls married into the service.

Brass buttons had nothing to do with it, Mamie knew.
Her feeling for Ike went far beyond externals. It was
compounded of such things as delight in his conversation and homespun humor, admiration for him as a person, and strong physical attraction, all of which added
up to a warm happy feeling of completeness when they
were together. Still she put off the moment of decision,

pushed the necessity for it to the back of her mind. It was so nice to drift.

Mr. and Mrs. Doud finally woke Mamie from her pleasant daze. They were watchful, anxious as devoted parents ever are. In addition, they were themselves undecided as to what they hoped Mamie would do. On the one hand, they were extremely fond of Ike. In truth, Mr. Doud had begun to regard him almost as the son he had always wanted. Certainly he was the finest young man who ever had paid attention to Mamie. There was no question about the strength of his feeling for her; he was transparently, chivalrously, totally in love. Shrewd businessman though he was, Mr. Doud took due cognizance of that. So genuine and deep an emotion was no light weight in the balance. On the other hand—there were so many things on the other hand.

That Ike came of very plain people was the least of these; the Douds were no snobs. That he had no money, and never would make any in the Army, was not a controlling factor, but it touched the scale; for who could tell if Mamie, who had butterflied it so gaily in lovely clothes and luxury, could stand the grind of comparative poverty? Knowing their daughter, the Douds thought she had the stuff it took. But if she did not, it would be pitiful to watch her break; it would be unfair to Ike.

Worst of all in the Douds' reckoning was that Ike was an Army man. That meant that Mamie would never have a home of her own. There would never be a friendly Lafayette Street where she could make a place for herself and know the security of permanence among old friends. *The whole Army would be Mamie's Lafayette Street*, but her parents could not foresee that. They envisioned, truly enough, the long succession of starkly adequate Army quarters and run-down rented houses, the many moving days, the anxieties of raising children on the run, the boredom of those small, introverted communities of Army posts; the lonely months when Army wives must wait and worry.

Reviewing the serenity and happiness of their own lives together, the Douds could not wish such a life for Mamie. Yet could they choose for her? In the end they decided they could not. Instead they paid her the highest compliment parents can offer their child. They put it up to her.

In a long talk with Mamie, Mr. Doud painted the picture as blackly as he could. She listened thoughtfully as he told her of the hardships she must expect, neither taking them lightly nor overwhelmed by them. Indeed, she had pondered them before. For all her gaiety and frivolity, Mamie had the strength of character to face facts. She knew now that she loved Ike. The question was, would she be good for him, would she be able to help him in his chosen career? It was so far beyond her experience that she could not even imagine what it would be like. She was no coward, but she was afraid that she might fail him.

Mr. Doud had one more point to make. "We may be drawn into this war in Europe," he said, "in which case Ike will be among the first to go. He may come back wounded, utterly shattered; he may not come back at all. You must think of that too, Mamie."

Strange though it may seem to a generation who have watched their soldier husbands and sons go off to three wars, Mamie had not thought of that. The war in Europe, incredible and terrible, seemed a million miles away from Texas. That it should reach even into her safe

Western home had been past imagining. Now it became a sinister possibility.

"Do you think we will have to fight, Pooh Bah?" she asked.

"Not even the President knows that," her father answered. "He is trying with all his strength of will and soul to keep us out, but events may be too much for him."

It was then that Mamie knew that she must marry Ike. Thus, if he went to war, she would somehow find the strength for waiting. The one unbearable thing would be never to have called him her own. Her qualms about her capabilities as an Army wife were stilled by that decision. She could do the necessary things because she must.

"I *will* make him a good wife," she said.

It was the real beginning of maturity.

Mamie made her decision in January, 1916, but Ike did not hear the good news until Valentine's Day, which was the next time he proposed. It was the most wonderful day of his life. It still is.

Mamie's first engagement ring was her own class ring with their initials engraved inside; this, for secrecy. A little later he gave her a round cluster of small diamonds.

The die cast, Mamie was as anxious to be married as she had been evasive in reaching a decision. She became acutely aware of the country's glacial drift toward war. It threatened from two sides: in Europe, where German underseas boats were ruthlessly sinking American ships; in Mexico, where the whirligig of revolution brought irresponsible bandit leaders to great power. Mamie read the papers now with intense concentration, anxious to understand the complexities of foreign policy, desperately trying to forecast the future.

No matter how much they like the man of her choice, parents are always anxious for their daughter to wait a while, to make sure. The Douds were no exception. However, Mamie could not wait. The terrible urgency of the times pressed upon her. If she could have Ike only for a little while, then the days were too precious to waste. Mr. Doud was firmly for a year's engagement, but Mrs. Doud understood her daughter's heart. Of course Mike and Buster were on her side. Victorian father or no, Pooh Bah could not withstand the pressure of all his women.

Mamie did not care how she was married so long as it was quickly. Mrs. Doud insisted on a real wedding with a bridal gown and a veil, flowers, a wedding cake, and music. "It will be only once for you, I know, Mamie," she said. "So we had better do it right."

As the early spring flushed the fields around San Antonio and set the flowers rioting in all its gardens, the Douds prepared to return to Denver. There was so much to do before the date, which was to be July 1, 1916.

11

The Wedding

THERE WAS CONSTERNATION IN DENVER WHEN THE NEWS
of Mamie's engagement reached town. Ex-beaux
mourned in the houses of their second-best girls, who
consoled them a mite gleefully. Although long faces
were the fashion among the gentlemen, the greatest dismay was, unexpectedly, among Mrs. Doud's—and Mamie's—older friends. They thought she was plumb crazy.

The reason for their chagrin lay in the almost forgotten mores of the last days of American serenity. During
the long peace the profession of soldiering had fallen
into disrepute. We were almost like the Chinese, who,
alone among the nations, relegated military men to the
lowest caste. There was some reason for this, since Americans wishfully had come to think of war as an ana-
chronistic relic of the barbarous past. Also, in our small
peacetime Army under the stultifying rule of seniority

an officer did not have to be brilliant to rise to his profession; he just had to live long enough and be careful
to do nothing. Even many of America's favorite military
heroes, Washington, Jackson, and more recently, Theo-
dore Roosevelt, had been gifted amateurs. Thus, Americans, especially in the Western states, were suspicious of
anyone who chose the profession of arms.

In that tradition lived the ladies of Lafayette Street.
For once they were all of one mind. Eileen's mother,
Mrs. Ewing; Mrs. Baker, who lived next door; Mrs. Sibley and Dean Manly's wife across the street; even wise
and tolerant Mrs. Will Bird, who once called Mamie,
"The finest young lady I have ever known," cackled
warnings like the sacred geese of Rome.

"An Army man!" they said. "A nobody from Kansas.
. . . He's called Ike something or other, an outlandish
name. . . . Why did Mamie pick him? Why did Elivera
let her? John Doud at least has sense. You'd think he
could do something. . . . That poor girl . . . Army life
. . . no money . . . no position . . . not even a home. . . .
Always batted about from pillar to post . . ."

That last was true, though they may be excused for not
foreseeing that the last post would have such stately pillars.

They were not malicious, even though they may have
enjoyed the chance to gossip and the inevitable human
satisfaction of watching others make an error. They
really loved Mamie, because, by unanimous testimony,
she had always been thoughtful and sweet to them; because she gave them that ultimate, rare tribute from
youth to age of really liking them. So their dismay was
genuine; their anxiety, truly felt. Of course, they had
not yet met Ike.

He came to Denver on leave in May. Mrs. Askling, sitting with Mrs. Bird on the latter's front porch, saw a husky figure in a tightly belted uniform and a brown, visored cap with gold insignia swing casually off the Eleventh Avenue car and march down the street looking up at the house numbers. They quivered like pointing bird dogs.

The next day Mamie, anxious to show Ike off, brought him to tea at the Birds'. It had turned warm, and they sat on the front porch with its brown linen swing, green wicker furniture, and the potted plant. Young Edward Bird was there, and his small friend, John Askling. The two little boys glowered at this strange man called Ike who had come to take their adored Mamie away. To them he looked as tall as the tower on Daniel and Fisher's Department Store.

However, Mrs. Bird was charmed. All her prejudices against the Army melted away in the warmth of Ike's smile. When they had gone she pronounced the edict that stilled the wagging tongues, if not the doubts, of Denver, "If Mamie Doud selects him, I would back her choice. Mamie knows what she is doing."

To set the final seal of her approval on the marriage, Mrs. Bird gave a card party in Mamie's honor. The round table in the dining room was splendid with fine silver and sparkling cut glass on an exquisite lace table cloth, which Mrs. Bird had made herself. The heaps of deviled ham-and-egg sandwiches were cut in the shapes of hearts, spades, clubs, and diamonds. The individual fruit salads of white grapes and bananas were covered with marshmallows mixed in whipped cream, sprinkled with nuts, and topped by a maraschino cherry. Dessert consisted of a rich array of cakes of Mrs. Bird's own baking.

Virtually all the ladies of Lafayette Street and its environs were there. They played a game, now lost to history but highly appropriate for the occasion, called military euchre.

Eisenhower always has luck with the weather. On D day the storm abated just in time to allow his troops to land through the roaring surf and scale the cliffs at Omaha Beach. In the Battle of the Bulge the sun burst through dense clouds and fog at the crucial moment to allow the Allied Air to smash the German Panzers while the sky above Bastogne blossomed in gaily colored parachutes carrying the supplies that saved its beleaguered garrison. The occasion of his inauguration as President of the United States was a lovely April day in the middle of January. Naturally his wedding day was absolutely perfect.

One of the handsome tropical uniforms Ike had bought when he thought he was going to the Philippines came in handy, starched and snowy white, brass buttons gleaming, trousers pressed to a razor's edge. On his shoulder straps gleamed the silver bars of a first lieutenant—he had been promoted that day. He arrived at the Douds too early for the ceremony. As he teetered nervously from foot to foot while Mamie dressed upstairs, Mr. Doud said, "For heaven's sake, Ike, take it easy and sit down!"

"I can't," he answered.

"Why not?"

His broad grin momentarily erased the worried frown. "Spoil the crease in my pants," he answered.

In her room, with the familiar bird's-eye maple furniture suddenly become as strange as though she had already gone away, Mamie carefully pulled her wedding dress of Chantilly lace over her head. Mrs. Doud eased it down while Buster and Mike hovered bright-eyed with excitement. Downstairs the rustle of arrivals and the rising buzz of conversation were punctuated by the *ping-ping-twang* and a ripple of scales as the harpist on the landing tuned her instrument.

Mamie's nerves were as tight as the *E* string. It was not that she was suffering the usual bridal doubts about marrying this man—she was as sure then as always—it was just that she wanted everything to be perfect. Ike's laughter booming through the floor boards stroked her nerves like a soothing hand. "I guess we're ready, Momma," she said.

As Mamie came down the stairs, the faces of all the people turned up toward her. The house seemed crowded, but there were really not many there, just family and their closest friends. She squeezed past the harpist, careful not to tear her dress. Pooh Bah, looking very solemn and distinguished in his frock coat and high winged collar, was standing at the foot of the stairs. Beyond she could see the parlor fireplace, banked with pink gladioli. Ike was waiting there. She went toward him, smiling happily.

More people came in for the reception after the wedding. Mamie and Ike received them, standing on the red carpet at the top of the stoop. It was very gay, with people spilling off the veranda and all over the lawn. The tinkling tunes of the harp seemed just the right accompaniment for a summer wedding. However, there was a dissonant diversion as Mamie's small boy friends, Bob Baker, Ed Bird, and John Askling, put on a sort of charivari by marching through the alley beating tin dishpans.

Soon it was time to cut the cake with Ike's shiny sword. The dining room was crowded now, with people sipping punch or coffee and eating little sandwiches and ice cream.

Mamie and Ike were ready to go, coming down the stairs. In the hall they were mobbed and kissed. The red carpet was a path to the Packard twin-six waiting at the curb with Lucius at the wheel. Mamie hugged all her family. Then she was running to the car in a shower of rice, jumping in. Ike thumped down on the seat beside her. Lucius roared the motor, and they started with a jerk.

So they drove away on the first lap of the long, incredible road they would travel together. The people watching them felt more sharply than usual the heart-sinking moment of departure, for Mamie had been very special to them.

A Denver matron, standing a little tearfully on the steps, summed up the sentiments of the irreconcilables in a valedictory mutter: "There goes Mamie. And she could have married *anybody* in Denver!"

12

The Battle of Abilene

BECAUSE OF THE TENSION ON THE MEXICAN BORDER AND the rising peril of war with Germany, Ike only had ten days' leave. He and Mamie spent a two-day honeymoon at Eldorado Springs in the mountains west of Denver. Then they took a train for Abilene, Kansas.

As the Union Pacific train rattled down the long slope of the plains, Mamie was more nervous than ever again in her life. The ordeal of entertaining kings, queens, prime ministers, and famous generals, or of facing the roaring mobs of Election Eve would never be so great as the prospect of meeting Ike's parents. For Mamie knew how close were Ike's family ties, and she felt that the success of her marriage depended on making the Eisenhowers like her. It was the first test of whether or not she could make Ike a good wife.

The hour could not have been worse. They were due

at Abilene at 4:00 A.M. As the train jerked out of the station at Salina on the last lap, Mamie wondered how anybody could be friendly at that hour. The other people in the car, trying to sleep or moodily staring at nothing, looked wan and sweaty under the dim yellow bulbs. She felt as grimy as they looked, drained of vitality, yet as jumpy as a cat in a thunderstorm. She almost screamed as the brakes went on and the conductor opened the door in a shower of cinders to shout raucously, "Abil-e-e-e-en!"

The station was dim and deserted. Ike gave all but one of their bags to the sleepy telegraph operator, and took Mamie's arm. "We've got to walk," he said gaily. "It isn't far."

They trudged up an empty street lined by rickety stores and warehouses, then crossed the tracks. Ike pointed to a dark mass with a high chimney sticking up among the stars. "That's the creamery where Dad works," he said. "He's chief superintendent now."

The street was wide and very dark under the maples. A sputtering gas lamp made a pool of bluish light at the corner. Ike turned her left, and marched confidently along in total darkness. It was so still you could hear the corn clicking as it grew.

"There's a light. They're up!" he shouted triumphantly.

Sure enough Mamie saw a pinpoint of light ahead. Ike walked so fast that she was almost running to keep up. They hurried across a little lawn, and Mamie smelt the heavy sweetness of honeysuckle. Reaching ahead of her, Ike pushed the side door open, and she stumbled into a little room crowded with pleasantly worn furniture bathed in the yellow light of a kerosene lamp.

Quite suddenly it was not hard or frightening at all. Ike's mother, looking just like her picture with big blue eyes and hair piled up on her head under a little mob-cap, was hugging her. David Eisenhower kissed her lightly on the cheek and squeezed her hand. They wanted to be friendly just as much as she did. Mamie knew it was all right.

Mrs. Eisenhower had coffee going on the stove. They sat around the kitchen table, talking like one family who has just been reunited. Only Ike's father was silent, but when Mamie looked at him she won his shy, sweet smile.

Then Ike's young brothers, Earl and Milton, sleep-touseled in pajamas, peeked in the door. "Come on in and meet Mamie!" Ike boomed.

Slowly and very shyly they came up to shake hands. Mamie jumped up and gave them both her hands. "Now I've got some brothers like I always wanted!" she said.

They did not get any sleep at all. The neighbors were invited for a formal wedding breakfast at nine o'clock.

David Eisenhower provided small corsages for Mamie and Ida. The guests all wore their best Sunday clothes and their party manners. The formality lasted just about 15 minutes. Then it broke down under Ike's rampaging high spirits, and Mamie's warm delight in meeting her husband's folks.

It was none of your niminy-piminy breakfasts. Scrambled eggs and ham, grown and cured on the Eisenhower's little farm. Piles of golden griddle cakes. Steaks for those who wanted them. Thick yellow cream for the home-grown peaches, and country butter for the hot biscuits. Mamie, who always ate heartily, stuffed herself, to Ida Eisenhower's great delight. She thought a girl with an appetite like that must be all right.

In Kansas in the summertime you must expect thunderstorms, maybe even a cyclone. A humdinger brewed up between Ike and Mamie before they had been married a week. The first small thunderhead showed above the horizon when Ike announced that he thought he'd walk down town and look up some of the boys. Mamie did not think too much of being left all afternoon in the hot little house, but she supposed men, even Ike, had to have some freedom. He promised, "I won't be long, Honey."

It was an endless afternoon under the heavy blanket of Kansas heat, so different from the crisp air of Denver. Mamie tried sitting in the parlor; that was insufferable. The kitchen with its coal stove was next door to Devil's Island. Finally she went up and lay on her bed in a pool of perspiration. She heard the boys come in. David Eisenhower returned from work. She got up and went downstairs. It would be cooler on the porch and she could see Ike coming.

Six o'clock was suppertime. Ike still was not home. Quite frantic, Mamie turned to Ida for comfort and support.

Ida was annoyingly philosophical. "I expect he's down to Joner Callahan's playing a little poker," she said.

"Have they got a phone?" Mamie demanded.

"Yes, but I wouldn't call."

"I would!" said Mamie, eyes flashing.

She got Ike easily. Mad as she was, it was a relief to hear his voice. Then what he said made her even madder.

It seemed he was sorry, but he was behind and couldn't leave for a while. Mamie would not take such nonsense. He was to come back this minute!

Ike was very patient. "You don't understand, Honey. I can't quit now. I'm loser."

"Come now or don't bother to come at all," Mamie stormed, and banged down the receiver.

"That will fetch him," she said a little smugly.

"Don't get too upset if it doesn't," Ida suggested.

It was past two o'clock when Ike finally came in. He tip-toed upstairs and opened the door of his room. "It took a while longer than I thought, but—" he began amiably. Behind him the door was slammed with a crash that shook the little house.

Just what happened in the guest bedroom after that, nobody knows but Ike and Mamie, and they won't tell. But according to the signs and symptoms observed by the rest of the family, it must have been a battle royal. The principals admit that it was the worst fight they ever had.

Like those perhaps less violent Kansas storms, it cleared the air. Ike was much too kind a person callously to cause distress to anybody, let alone a person he loved so dearly. He learned about women that night—the fundamental facts that a small thing may hurt them more than a great one, and that, while you can be firm with a wife, maybe even a mite selfish, you can't be casual.

Mamie also learned a few things that she never forgot. She had the kind of sense that could be realistic even with herself. She admitted to herself that she was "a spoiled brat"—spoiled not so much by her parents, though they had given her a wonderful life, as by her beaux who had trembled with fear at her frown. A husband, she learned—at least this Ike—could not be bullied. She always says that was when she made up her mind that her husband was the head of the house. In her heart she was glad.

So the Battle of Abilene was one of those rare encounters in which both sides gain something. Certainly it is a fortunate marriage when the first fight is the worst.

13

Army Life

ARMY LIFE WAS NOT SO BAD AS PEOPLE SAID, MAMIE DE-cided in those first months at Fort Sam. It is true that their quarters were pretty cramped. Ike was the junior officer on the post; as such he rated two bare rooms and a bath. There was only one closet. The furniture, according to Mamie, was "horrible"—some old government chairs with leather seats that Ike managed to borrow, and a kitchen table.

But Mamie had a walnut bedroom suite and some nice wedding presents including an exquisite little oriental rug. She rented a piano for five dollars a month. Most important of all was the fact that Mamie had the ability to put her signature on any place she inhabited. No matter how unpromising the quarters, she could make them look lived in, make them a home. So they were comfortable, and the windows looked out on the fine green lawns of the old fort.

Very cautiously they began to buy additional things they needed, always paying cash. Mamie was adamant about not going into debt, which is what she considered installment buying.

Ike may have been head of the house, but Mamie was Secretary of the Treasury. On the first day of their first month together, Ike turned over his pay check to her. That was the pattern he followed always, never questioning what she did with the money. He hated shopping and even tried to make Mamie buy his clothes. She was willing to get shirts, neckties, underwear, and handkerchiefs, but at one point she rebelled. "You've got to buy your own suits," she said. "I can't try on trousers for you."

The way Mamie managed their finances was proof that Pooh Bah had taught her well. It also showed that she had a head firmly fixed on her shoulders and the ability to do anything she put her mind to. Never in all their lives did she get into debt, though sometimes by the end of the month her bank balance was down to two figures —on the wrong side of the decimal point.

It was easy enough at first. Ike's promotion to first lieutenant raised his pay to $161.67 a month. It seemed like riches to them, and, indeed, it was many years before they again had so much extra cash to spend. This was because their overhead was extremely low. Ike had all those new uniforms. Mamie had her trousseau. There was no rent to pay, and they could eat at the Officers' Mess for $30 a month. That left a handsome sum that was pure gravy.

There were, however, serious disadvantages; for example, the little red ants, who met Mamie on the very threshold of her married life.

The Eisenhowers each had bought an enormous, old-fashioned wardrobe trunk. Ike still uses his. As the trunks were being closed that last hurried day in Denver, a present of a fine fruit cake arrived. Mamie popped it into a drawer of her trunk and sent it on its way.

While she and Ike visited at Abilene, the trunks went on to Fort Sam, where they were placed on the veranda of their quarters, there to stand waiting for nearly ten days. When she arrived and opened the fruit cake drawer a squeak of horror startled Ike. The cake was literally pullulating with ants.

Mamie gingerly picked the thing up, and was about to throw it as far as she could, when an old Army wife intervened. "Don't throw it away," she said. "Just stand it in the sunshine and all the little ants will go away."

Mamie followed her advice. The ants followed their sun-hating nature, and the Eisenhowers ate their fruit cake after all.

Mamie had led a life sheltered from insects in almost bugless Denver, and had lived in San Antonio only in winter. The tropical Texas summer found her embattled against hordes of cockroaches, flies, and those omnipresent ants. Everything edible had to be hermetically sealed. So much as a crumb on the floor brought the tiny invaders marching in batallion front. The price of liberty —from ants—was, indeed, eternal vigilance. When the Eisenhowers' Texas friends sent them several boxes of candy, the problem became acute. Mamie solved it by hanging the boxes by their ribbons from the ugly brass chandelier in the parlor, making it look like a weird sort of Christmas tree, but effectively foiling the ants.

Though Mamie won the battle of the ants, Ike lost to the mosquitoes. Not at Fort Sam, where they were well under control, but on a practice march with the regiment, he became the target for the day of a wing of stegomyia anopheline. He returned to Mamie with his face looking like a bad case of measles. What he caught, however, was malaria.

That ended the Eisenhowers' practice of eating out. Mamie had enjoyed the pleasantly casual atmosphere of the mess but even she was tired of mess-cooked food. Now Ike felt too ill to go to mess; furthermore, he never liked to take a meal out if he could get home cooking. That brought up the question of who would home-cook it. Mamie says that she was very expert at making fudge, so Ike took over.

Mamie bought a little wooden icebox which she set up in the bathroom. Naturally she often forgot to empty the pan underneath as the ice melted. Her derelictions would be called to her attention by a tide of water seeping under the bathroom door and spreading across the parlor.

She also rigged up an electric grill, a hot plate, and a chafing dish, and Ike did the rest. It was fun eating off their pretty wedding-present china and the bridal silver. Because Mamie was eager to learn for her husband's sake, her cooking soon became rather better than adequate, but she never acquired Ike's artistry. Nor did she attempt his two specialties, steaks and vegetable soup.

As Ike made it, the soup was a three-day job. First he made the stock and set it to cool. The second day he scraped off the grease, then cooked up a batch of vegetables in it until they were virtually dissolved into their elements. On the third day he put in fresh vegetables, cooked them for no more than half an hour, and served. It was a wonderful brew.

In other ways Mamie conscientiously set herself to be a good Army wife. This involved learning the protocol of life on the post. It was an intricate pattern, built up through more than a century of Army regulations, plus the even more important unwritten customs of the service, some of which came all the way down from eighteenth-century usage of the British colonial troops. The basis of the whole business was Rank with a capital R. Mamie learned that the wife of a major—even though she were pock-marked, snaggle-toothed, and almost totally illiterate—was *ipso facto* a much more important person than the beautiful young bride of a first lieutenant. For an officer's record, that secret, sacred dossier of his whole life in the service on which depends promotion and opportunity, is written by his superiors. And what they think of him is often, though probably unwittingly, based to a considerable extent on how their wives feel toward his wife.

Mamie realized that with her pretty clothes and her youthful good looks—she had no false modesty—she must walk especially carefully among the older wives lest she irretrievably damage her husband's career. To her eternal credit, she accepted the situation with the becoming humility of a novice. Add to her pleasant deference to the older women the fact that she really liked almost everybody and showed it in her generous, unaffected way, and you have the answer to why the natural suspicion of an interloper thawed to genuine liking for her. According to the testimony of many men and women, both older and younger than she, she became one of the most popular women in the Army.

The young Eisenhowers went out a good deal during that first winter. Fort Sam was a gay post, and in addition there were Mamie's friends in San Antonio. To repay people, they first tried giving a series of dinners at the St. Anthony or the Majestic Hotel. Somehow such parties were never satisfactory to them. Entertaining in hotels seemed a sterile sort of hospitality. So they switched to extremely informal little buffet suppers in their quarters. Those gay Sunday evening suppers, with Mamie playing the rented piano and everybody singing at the top of his lungs—and what, if Ike was three keys down?—were so successful that they produced Mamie's basic maxim in entertaining: "Most people would rather have hash in your home than pheasant in a restaurant."

Because of its friendly atmosphere and warm hospitality, Ike and Mamie's little apartment became known at the Fort as Club Eisenhower. It was the first of a whole

series of Club Eisenhowers throughout every part of the
world where Ike's career took them.

Mamie's indoctrination into Army life, though comparatively easy, was not all peaches and cream. Behind
the normal routine life and the pleasant round of simple
gaieties loomed the steadily darkening shadow of war.
As Germany intensified her submarine campaign in defiance of the comity of nations and President Wilson's
grave warnings, the dreaded question became not if, but
when.

Even before war was declared, Mamie had her share
of anxiety and waiting. At the end of August Ike was
ordered on detached duty as inspector-instructor of mili-
tia on the Mexican Border. His bailiwick was the Illinois
National Guard at Camp Travis, Texas. By rising at
dawn, he could commute to his post in a little roadster
that Pappa Doud gave him; but many a night he did not
get home until midnight or not at all.

Even when Ike was at Fort Sam, Mamie could not
always feel easy. Because of our strained relations with
Mexico, while the National Guard lined the long arid
border and General Pershing led American troops
through Chihuahua in pursuit of the bandit leader,
Pancho Villa, the Mexican population of San Antonio
was unusually turbulent. Military police constantly
patroled the streets.

One night when Ike had this duty, he was leading a
patrol on Matamoros Street, which was the sinkhole of
the city. He marched briskly down the narrow roadway
lined by somber, darkened houses that seemed deserted
until a splash of light through a slatting blind or a shriek
muffled by adobe walls hinted at the volcanic life within.

Suddenly his sergeant jerked him backward. At the same instant came the crack of a rifle and a bullet zipped angrily past his nose.

The sharp-eyed sergeant, seeing an armed man lurking in a doorway, had saved Ike's life. Although Ike led the shouting patrol in swift pursuit, the man vanished into the rabbit warren behind the blank façades of the houses. Oddly enough, considering his profession, this was the only time Ike was under fire until he landed in Algiers as commander-in-chief of the Allied invasion forces in World War II.

Though he had intended not to tell Mamie, Ike looked so excited when he came in that she knew something had happened, and with her quickly acquired wifely expertness she soon pried the truth out of him. After that she slept no more when he was on night patrol.

Another cause for anxiety was Ike's wish to take the flying course being given for officers at the old Balloon School in San Antonio. Mamie hated airplanes then and, indeed, for most of her life until she finally had to get used to them. She had vowed to herself never to interfere in Ike's career, but this was different. She was not going to have him risking his neck in those miserable little contraptions of wood and canvas tied together with piano wire. And she had an ace up her sleeve to stop him.

When he finally announced his determination to apply for the course, she announced with even firmer finality that she was going to have a baby. Ike joyfully surrendered.

All these worries were minor compared to the awful imminence of war. Throughout the month of March,

1917, Germany was clearly winning on the continent as weary French and British armies staggered backward under the terrible mass attacks of the Wehrmacht and the U-boats ranged the winter seas, sinking every ship they sighted. Mamie knew that it could only be a matter of days before America must accept the challenge of barbarism. She did not question the hard necessity or harass Ike with her anxiety. But dread lay like a cold lump in her stomach.

The pleasant life at Fort Sam ended abruptly on April 1, 1917, when Lieutenant Eisenhower was ordered to join the Fifty-seventh Infantry training at Leon Springs, Texas. There was no place for women in that hastily built encampment. So Mamie remained in the suddenly empty little apartment at the Fort.

The following evening, April 2, 1917, President Woodrow Wilson solemnly asked Congress to declare war on Germany saying: "The day has come when America is privileged to spend her blood and might for the principles that gave her birth and happiness and the peace which she has treasured. God helping her she can do no other."

Unbearably lonely those nights on the double bed in her little room, Mamie never doubted that the President had spoken the truth. America could indeed do no other. So she tried to brace herself for the long ordeal. But she wept a little in spite of herself. It would have been so much easier to take this news if Ike had been with her.

14

Partners at Gettysburg

MAMIE'S LONELINESS IN HER FIRST REAL SEPARATION
from her husband led her to a rather desperate act.
There was Ike, only 27 miles away at Leon Springs, but
so held by the pressure of wartime work that he could
not get off to see her. And there was the Douds' new
Pierce Arrow sitting in the garage back of the house on
McCullough Street. The hitch was that, though Mamie
had learned to drive Creepy with its steering tiller, single control, and one brake peddle, she had not the faint-
est idea how to manage a real automobile. That did not
stop her.

On a Saturday afternoon early in May she went to
her father's house, the blank windows of which proclaimed it closed for the summer, to reconnoiter. She
hailed a neighbor and got him to give her a quick lesson
in the intricacies of the formidable brass gear shift

and emergency brake, and the clutch, brake, and gas peddles. The next morning she was up at dawn ready for her deed of derring-do.

It was only six o'clock in the morning, with the red sun stretching the shadows long across the misty grass, and the cool of the night still in the air. McCullough Street was sound asleep. Mamie opened the garage doors and climbed to the high leather seat of the Pierce Arrow. Her feet barely touched the peddles; the wooden steering wheel seemed immense. She started the engine in two or three tries. As the car trembled with power she sat quaking with fear. Very cautiously she maneuvered the gear shift into what she hoped was reverse. It was, and the great car backed slowly into the empty street. With a horrible clash of gears, Mamie shifted into first while it was still moving backward, and was off on her wobbling way.

She had planned well, for there was hardly a person in sight on all the road to Leon Springs—a lucky thing for them. Mamie knew the road, and never once had to stop until she came to the gates of the camp. There stood Ike, warned ahead of time, peering anxiously down the road. He saw the car coming very slowly and uncertainly. Mamie, wild-eyed, stuck her head around the windshield and yelled, "Jump in quick, Ike! I don't know how to stop!"

Ike was not long at Leon Springs, but he made some fine friends there, Johnny Walker, now Major General John Walton Walker, and Art Nevins, an engineer fresh out of Officers Training Camp, who stayed in the Army to become Brigadier General Arthur S. Nevins, and Ike's lifelong friend and adviser.

Like every officer of the Regular Army—and most of the volunteers, too—Ike was frantic to get overseas. He was Regimental Supply Officer of the Fifty-seventh. On July 1, he was promoted to captain and expected to go with his regiment when they sailed for France. Instead, on September 20, 1917, he was ordered to the Officers Training Camp at Fort Oglethorpe, Georgia.

It was a bitter blow to him, and to Mamie as well. Just three days later her son was born, and Ike was not there to see him. However, Poppa and Mamma Doud came rushing down from Denver to greet their first grandchild. He was christened Doud Dwight Eisenhower. But Mamie called him Icky.

Poppa, still "quick with the checkbook," gave Mamie an allowance of $100 a month from that time on.

Fort Oglethorpe, expanded to ten times its normal compliment, with thousands of trainees in flimsy wooden barracks and their wives fighting for accommodations in the town, was no place for a mother with a young baby, so Mamie stayed on in San Antonio. On December 1, Ike got another disappointment—orders to Fort Leavenworth, Kansas, as instructor to provisional officers at the Army service schools. He was too good at teaching men for his own good—or so he felt, wondering if he ever would get to France.

What he considered the final blow to his career fell when, on March 1, 1918, he was appointed to command the Tank Corps at Camp Colt, Gettysburg, Pennsylvania. It was, he knew, a sign of great confidence for so young an officer, a mere captain, to be put in command of a training center which at its peak held 30,000 men. But it was not war. And how could an officer who had taken no part in the battles in France, who had never heard a shot fired in anger, hope to rise in a postwar army?

Furthermore, though his intelligence told him that he was serving his country as he best could—and he had no choice in the matter anyhow—he somehow felt that he was shirking the danger and the dirt, the hardships and terrors, that his fellow cadets of just three years ago were facing so gallantly. Ike was most unhappy.

Mamie was delighted. Now she could be with Ike again.

When she broke camp at Fort Sam to start the long trek that was to take her through 35 moves in 35 years, Mamie did a very foolish thing. One of her older friends said, "You'll be always on the move, don't clutter up your life with a lot of *things*. Travel light."

On this advice, Mamie sold her pretty bedroom furniture, the rug and all the other pieces she had acquired. About $900 worth of furniture went for $99. For years afterward, in shoddy rented houses and bare government quarters, Mamie regretted her decision.

The Eisenhowers rented a charming, old, furnished house on Springs Avenue in Gettysburg. It was built of the dark red brick typical of the town and had watched the Confederate and Union Armies surge up and down that broad, shady street in the heat and terror of those July days in 1863.

Once again Gettysburg was full of troops, boys in khaki with high-collared, close-buttoned tunics, leather puttees, and the cowboy hats that would be exchanged for the cocky new overseas caps only when they got their orders for France. As the wife of their commanding officer, Mamie felt very close to them; like the Peacock Academy football team, they were "Ike's boys."

If Captain Eisenhower was faced with responsibilities beyond his years and rank, so was twenty-year-old Mamie. The Commanding Officer's wife had to entertain all the top brass, the big-shot politicos, and the important industrialists who came to inspect Camp Colt. A great many came, for here was an experiment unique in the annals of the American Army. Tanks had been invented by the British and used in warfare for the first time a little over two years before, when six clumsy experimental models had lumbered through the mud on the Somme front at four miles per hour to change the whole technique of war. Everyone wanted to see how the American forces were being trained for this startling innovation.

Mamie welcomed the generals and senators, the cabinet secretaries, and the presidents of corporations to her house, and gave them the best food she could fix up. She was not overawed—maybe she did not know enough about their importance to be—so she treated them as welcome friends, and, being Mamie, really liked them. So, of course, they had a good time and remembered her long after she and Ike had lapsed back into the comparative obscurity of Army routine. Naturally, those who were still alive recalled her even more vividly when the great things began to happen to Ike. There was always, both before he became famous and afterward, a sort of glow in their memories that Mamie's unaffected friendliness had engendered.

Meanwhile Ike was having a terrible time with the Tank Corps. Thousands of young men had volunteered for this service, which was supposed to be a *corps d'élite*. They were eager to learn the techniques of modern mechanized warfare; they were brimming with élan. Nobody could ask for a finer group of men to command, Ike knew. The only trouble was that he had no tanks!

At first, indeed, he did not even have quarters or supplies for the half-trained men who arrived in the long troop trains. They pitched their khaki tents in the Wheat Field where the last Confederate charge at Gettysburg had wilted under the terrible fire from the Union troops on the gentle, wooded hills beyond. It was bitterly cold in March, and Ike's boys crouched around small campfires miserable and unfed, for the expected rations did not arrive. Ike was with them until late every night, sending out foraging parties to buy food from the farmers and straw, which was warmer than cots to sleep in. He bolstered his men's morale by telling them frankly what had gone wrong and how he was trying to remedy it.

When he got home, cold and weary, he paced the parlor floor, talking to Mamie indignantly about "those poor hungry boys."

Such conditions could be remedied, and were, very quickly. The tank problem was another matter.

Arguments about tank construction between the Bureau of Ordnance and civilian manufacturers, and changes in design even after the machine tools had been set up, so delayed production that not one American tank ever got to France in World War I; they were just beginning to trickle off the assembly lines when the armistice was signed. The single American tank brigade that saw action under Colonel George S. Patton, Jr., was equipped with French tanks.

After some months Ike finally got a tank, a French Renault type called a "Whippet," capable of carrying two men. With that he was supposed to teach 30,000 men about tank warfare.

Thus Major Eisenhower—he had been promoted to temporary rank on June 1, 1918—had two tremendous problems. First, he had to devise a system of training troops in the use of something that was not there, and secondly, to keep up the morale of men who had ex-

pected so much and found so little. Mamie's problem was to keep up the morale of Major Eisenhower. That they succeeded was proof of extraordinary qualities in them both.

The system of theoretical training plus field maneuvers with imaginary tanks that Ike devised was so successful that Colonel Patton, who received his trainees in France, was able to lead them into battle after a minimum of instruction with the real thing. At Camp Colt the men feeling that they were really gaining knowledge, responded to Ike's quality of leadership by giving him their best.

As for Mamie, she matured magnificently. Sharing her husband's frustrations and anxieties, joking him out of discouragement, restoring his weary body in the fine old-fashioned way of feeding him good food and providing a warm and happy home to come back to, she played her full part. Very tardily—in fact six years later, so slowly do the mills of the Army grind—Ike was awarded the Distinguished Service Medal with this citation:

> *While commanding officer of the Tank Corps Training Center, he displayed unusual zeal, foresight, and marked administrative ability in organizing, training, and preparation for overseas of technical troops of the Tank Corps.*

Ike certainly deserved it, but perhaps young Mamie, the erstwhile butterfly of Denver, who learned so quickly how to entertain the Very Important, take care of a young baby, and comfort and fortify a husband, ought to have had a citation too.

The months at Gettysburg made a real partnership out of the Eisenhowers' marriage. At Fort Sam they had still been honeymooners, and during the first year of war Ike had been away at the different camps. But at Camp Colt, where Mamie shared her husband's problems and successes, they became the team they have been ever since.

Mamie even learned a little about the technical side of Ike's profession. On Sunday afternoons he liked to drive with her around the old battlefield, explaining the disposition of the forces on those two queerly named ranges of hills, Seminary Ridge and Cemetery Ridge. He pointed out where Lee had made his fatal errors and where Union General Meade had gotten a lucky break. At first Mamie only pretended to be interested, but Ike's explanations were so clear and his descriptions so vivid that she began almost to *see* the lines of gray-clad, yelling men, their long bright bayonets flashing in the July sun, come swarming down into the valley, and the dark-blue Union troops crouching behind the stone walls, shooting and shooting and finally meeting the Confederate charges in hand-to-hand melee. What is more, she began to understand the intricate pattern of the battle, and the reasons for the different maneuvers. Most important of all, she came to understand her husband so well that she could even *feel* as he did.

It was natural to rejoice when Ike was promoted to lieutenant colonel (temporary) on October 14, 1918. The next test was harder.

It was about November 1, and she was watching for Ike as she always did in the late afternoon. When she saw him swinging gaily up Springs Avenue under the maple leaves bright gold in the autumn sunset, she knew he had good news. He slammed in the door and strode into the room, waving official papers in his hand, eyes brilliant blue, cheeks glowing with happiness.

"My orders for France have come!" he said. "I go November eighteenth."

Mamie had dreaded this moment so long, had anticipated a thousand times how her heart would sink and her whole inner self crumble.

Nothing of the sort happened. So close had she and Ike become that, for this first moment at least, she felt only joy in his happiness.

"I'm so glad, Ike," she said. And she meant it.

15

Down Grade

IKE NEVER WENT TO FRANCE. THE ARMISTICE THAT ended the terrible four years of mass slaughter was signed on November 11, 1918. He was truly glad it was all over, for he is one of the few professional soldiers who hate war with all their hearts. But, as he went to Camp Dix where, according to his orders, he should have embarked, he could not shake off a sense of frustration. As Monsieur Beaucaire said in the play of the same name, "All those years of training, and not one *leetle* fight!"

Those were sad days for Mamie, despite her relief at the ending of the war. On November 6, she had received word at Gettysburg that Buster, who had been ill of an infection of the kidneys, was very much worse. Taking Icky, she started immediately for San Antonio. When her train reached Chicago, a telegram told her that Buster was dead.

Feeling terribly alone, she changed her destination to Denver, where Buster was buried in the family plot. Her unhappy father and mother told of the light-hearted courage with which Buster had fought her illness, and how to the very last day she had worked knitting helmets and socks for the soldiers. On November 7, the day when a false report of an armistice had set off premature rejoicing throughout the nation, they had told Buster the war was over. That afternoon she died.

Mamie stayed in Denver while Ike was at Camp Dix, and from December 22, 1918, to March 15, 1919, at Camp Benning, Georgia. She had to do something to relieve her loneliness and boredom so, womanlike, she

changed her hairdo, cutting the famous bangs. It was a lucky thing for her that, when he saw them, Ike approved!

In March, Eisenhower was ordered to Camp Meade,

Maryland, commanding the Heavy Tank Brigade. Mamie
and Icky joined him there.

In their bare, barnlike quarters at Camp Meade,
Mamie longed for her pretty furniture. There was literally nothing in the apartment, which was flimsily parti-
tioned off in what had been a barracks. Ike found some
broken-down furniture on the camp dump and fixed it
up so it was at least sitable. Mamie made a dressing
table and bench out of some packing boxes covered with
cretonne. They slept on two Army cots obtained from
the quartermaster's stores, and cooked over an oil stove
in an unused shower room. In spite of all that, their
quarters became a Club Eisenhower.

That Mamie was still somewhat unsophisticated in the
ways of the Army is shown by a story of this time that
she tells on herself. The Secretary of War, inspecting
Camp Meade, stopped by the Eisenhower's quarters,
while Ike was on duty in the field. Making polite conversation, the Secretary asked, "What does your husband do best, Mrs. Eisenhower?"

Mamie answered brightly, "He plays an awfully good
game of poker."

When Ike heard about it, he asked, between despair
and laughter, "What possessed you to say such a thing
to the Secretary, Mamie?"

Big-eyed and innocent, Mamie replied, "I took it for
granted he knew you were a good soldier."

Almost the first people the Eisenhowers met at Meade
were Colonel and Mrs. George S. Patton, Jr., who became their firm friends. Ike looked up to Patton with
respect tinged with unrancorous envy. Georgie had done
all the things Ike had wanted to do. As American Observer, he had taken part in the great British tank attack

at Cambrai in December, 1917, when the German lines had been smashed by hundreds of lumbering, fire-breathing monsters. He had commanded the only American-manned tanks in the war at the Battles of Saint-Mihiel and the Argonne. In the latter he had been wounded and left for dead on the field, only to revive in a sulphurous rage when he found himself laid out ready for the burial squad. Georgie was a tall, thin man with a big nose and burning blue eyes. His uniforms were exquisitely tailored, his spurred cavalry boots glistened, and his chest was chromatic with ribbons won for valor. His intense absorption in military science, combined with imaginative audacity, made him perhaps the most brilliant young officer in the Army. And he had a delightful, though bawdy, sense of humor.

In his turn, Patton respected Eisenhower for his ability, proven by the well-trained men who had come from Camp Colt to join the American Tank Brigade.

Mamie liked the colonel's lady immensely. Bea Patton had two young daughters, one of them about Icky's age. She looked pretty and plump and comfortable. Actually she was a little gamecock of a woman, completely imbued with Georgie's do-or-die spirit and afraid of nothing on earth.

In their personal characteristics and tastes no two couples could have been more opposite than the Eisenhowers and Pattons. Georgie was extremely temperamental, domineering, and picturesquely profane; Ike easy-going, gentle, and almost puritanicallly clean of speech. Bea was an ardent sportswoman with wide interests; Mamie, at this stage in her development, was absorbed in her child and her home. Yet, perhaps because of these very differences, they were extremely congenial.

The two men had the bond of ambition and mutual interest in their profession. They were both taking correspondence courses from the General Staff School at Fort Leavenworth, and it became their custom to do their homework together at the quarters of one or the other. These sessions were very profitable to both, for their dissimilar minds reacted to spur each other on. When the lessons were done, they talked about the tank tactics of the future. Many years later these discussions and the mutual understanding they produced were immensely valuable to their country.

While the men talked shop, Mamie and Bea found plenty of things to discuss, and each enjoyed exploring the refreshing personality of the other.

During the summer of 1919, Ike went as observer on the first transcontinental trip of a truck convoy. The idea was to see if the trucks could make it. They did, but in not much better time than covered wagons. Ike was gone for over seven weeks. When he got back, he resumed his studies in the Officer Tank School. There were plenty of real tanks now for him to practice with—French, British, captured German, and our own tardy product of Dayton's production lines.

Since there was a surplus of high-ranking officers in the vanishing peacetime Army, Ike was demoted from his temporary rank of lieutenant colonel to major (temporary) on July 1, 1920, and returned to his permanent grade of captain on November 4, 1920. This reduced the Eisenhower's income by almost a third. Money never worried Ike, but Mamie had some trouble cutting her shrinking cloth to fit their necessities.

In the summer of 1920 Ike was due for leave, so he took Icky and Mamie to visit the Douds in Denver. Mamie found it wonderful to be home. After the lush but tame Maryland countryside, the sweep and clarity of her beloved plains and the uncompromising grandeur of the Rockies were a refreshing draught of beauty. The house on Lafayette Street seemed especially comfortable after those barren quarters at Meade, and being waited on was certainly an agreeable change. Once again Mamie sat on the red carpet, this time with Ike grinning amiably up at her, and her old friends came to renew former ties.

It would have been quite perfect except for the pigeons. A whole flock of them had strayed from some distant cote and taken up quarters in the back yard. They whirled and circled over the house, and were habitually casual about their manners. Mamie's chosen spot became somewhat perilous.

"I'll fix them," Ike volunteered.

He found the shotgun he had bought as a boy stored in the attic, and with this anti-aircraft armament went forth to battle. Lucius caught up a tea tray and followed him into the back yard.

They made quite a picture, Ike with his gun at the ready, Lucius, tall and dignified, standing behind him with the tray. Each time Ike's gun cracked, a pigeon fell. While he reloaded, Lucius retrieved the bird and, putting it on the tray, returned impassively to his station. The front stoop was soon safe for company.

Camp Meade in the rainy autumn days seemed more dismal than ever to Mamie. The Pattons had been transferred to Fort Myer. Both Ike and Mamie missed their stimulating company. However, Christmas was coming.

Mamie intended to make it very special for Icky; now that he was three, he could really enjoy it. She had great fun buying him presents, the most resplendent of which was the tiniest tricycle made.

Two days before Christmas she went to Baltimore with other Army wives to buy presents for the Christmas tree for the enlisted men's children. When she got home, the woman who was taking care of Icky told her that the child seemed feverish. Mamie immediately got the camp doctor, who said Icky had a bad cold.

Christmas day was sad. Icky, hot and fretful, was kept in bed, with only a glimpse of his Christmas tree, waiting all shiny with tinsel and stars and real candles in the parlor. Mamie was developing a heavy cold, and when she was not taking care of Icky, she lay in her room with a migraine headache. Ike, moving from one to the other, was valiantly cheerful.

Two days later Icky's face turned crimson, and his temperature soared. The doctor gave the frightening verdict: scarlet fever.

Three decades later, with the discovery of sulpha drugs, little Icky would have been in no danger, but in 1920 scarlet fever was the most dreaded plague of childhood. An ambulance came to take Icky to the post hospital. Mamie, with a high fever herself, was dressed and ready to go. But the doctor feared that she might have caught the disease and ordered her into quarantine.

For a dreadful week Mamie was forced to stay at home while her son fought for his life. Everything that medicine knew then was brought to help him. The greatest specialist in the country came from Johns Hopkins to stand almost helpless beside his cot. Ike was at the hospital day and night. It was no use. On January 2, 1921, Icky died in his father's arms.

Mamie never knew how she withstood the terrible train ride to Denver as she brought her son home. Somewhere she found the courage to go through the heart-breaking business. And Ike was with her. Harrowing though his own experience had been, he still had a reserve of strength to lend her. By the force of his love and tenderness he carried her through her morass of misery.

To this day he has never forgotten to send Mamie flowers on Icky's birthday.

16

Locks and Bats

THE EISENHOWERS SPENT ANOTHER DREARY YEAR AT
Camp Meade. It was a time of discouragement and drift.
Mamie was lost and unhappy. The miserable little apartment seemed the loneliest place in the world when Ike
was not there. Thank God, some kindly friends had
taken Icky's toys away before she came back from Denver, but the place was still full of him.

Even Ike was despondent. Pacifist sentiment in America was reducing the Army to a mere skeleton force.
There remained little incentive for ambition and little
hope for the future. If he were lucky, Ike could look
forward to the dead end of being retired as a colonel,
which made him wonder if he had not made an awful
mistake in choosing this career, and if he might not yet
recoup by taking a job in civilian life. Only nobody
offered him a job.

On January 8, 1922, Ike was graduated from Officer Tank School, commanding the Three-hundred-first Tank Battalion. Now, at last, a break came in their period of stagnation. It was due indirectly to Georgie Patton.

Almost two years before, Patton's close friend, Major General Fox Connor, at that time Chief of Staff to the disbanding American Expeditionary Force, had paid a visit to Camp Meade. Patton made a point of introducing Ike to him, and indubitably told him of their studies together and his respect for Eisenhower's ability. Fox Connor took a hard look at the young officer, liked what he saw, and made a mental note.

Late in 1921, General Connor was given command of the Twentieth Infantry in the Panama Canal Zone with the directive to revamp the defenses of the Canal to meet the threat of the Air Age. He needed a good man as his executive officer, so he wrote to Eisenhower.

When Ike received the letter, his enthusiasm revived. However, he first asked Mamie if she would mind a tour of duty in the tropics. She stuck to her principles. "It's up to you, Ike," she said. "I'll go wherever is best for you."

A few days after Ike's graduation from the tank school they sailed in an Army transport for the Canal Zone.

Camp Gaillard, where the Twentieth Infantry was stationed, was at the Culebra Cut—which the French called Gaillard—near the Pacific end of the Canal. The Eisenhowers reached it early one afternoon, driving out from the Pedro Miguel locks on a dirt road between the Canal and the jungle in a Model-T Ford, which was the jeep of World War I. General and Mrs. Connor greeted them with friendly warmth and took them to see their new quarters.

One of Mamie's favorite sayings is, "I've lived in everything from shacks with cracks to palaces." The house at Gaillard was one of the oddities of her collection. It had been built by the French more than thirty years before, when Count Ferdinand de Lesseps, having conquered the Isthmus of Suez, was fighting a losing battle against heat and yellow fever to drive a canal across the much tougher Isthmus of Panama. The house stood on stilts near the edge of the cleared fields on a bluff above the Canal. It was two stories high, made of thin planking with a sheet-iron roof that fairly vibrated in the heat of the tropical sun. The rather spacious rooms were jungle dim at noon, for galleries ran all around the house on both floors to keep out the glare. Since it is always hot in Panama, the windows had no glass but were protected by lattices and wire screens.

That first night the Eisenhowers had dinner at the Officers' Mess and met many of the men and women who were to be their closest friends for the next two years. When the sun set suddenly behind the round, jungle-covered hills, the soaking, sodden heat was blown away by a puff of cool air, and by the time they reached their new home it seemed almost cold by comparison.

As she got ready for bed, Mamie wondered why the legs of their Army cots stood in little tins of kerosene. She soon found out, for these small petroleum moats were inadequate protection against the omnipresent bed-bugs. Each week the cots had to be taken out and flamed.

As soon as the lights were put out, Mamie became un-happily aware of the weird wild sounds that filled the night. A hundred feet away the neat clipped lawn of the house was cut short by the tangled curtain of primeval jungle. Behind it prolific tropical life pursued its nocturnal affairs with squeals, squawks, howls, growls and the subhuman chittering of monkeys. To these presently was added a sound like a saw rasping on the timbers of the house.

Mamie shot bolt upright in bed. "What's that, Ike?" she squeaked. "It's eating the house."

"Probably a rat," her husband answered soothingly. "We've just got to ignore these things or we won't get any sleep at all."

This was good advice, but it took practice; there were so many things to ignore. Besides the jungle sounds and the bedbugs, there were cockroaches as big as hummingbirds, all sorts of spiders, a few snakes, and a complete collection of lizards. Mamie dared not use a white tablecloth because it would soon be black with ants.

Worst of all, to Mamie's thinking, were the bats. The bats were not natives of Panama. The French had imported them in the hope that they would eat the swarms of yellow-fever mosquitoes, who were more deadly than an army with repeating rifles. For their aerial allies, the French had built curiously shaped towers, where the bats hung by their feet in hundreds. They also passed a law making it a crime to kill a bat. Though American Army engineers had long since eliminated the mosquitoes, the law stayed on the books.

One of these bat towers stood near the Eisenhowers' quarters. As Mamie says, "The trouble was that the bats seemed to like my home better than theirs." Each evening at dusk, they swirled out of the tower in a darting, squeaking cloud, and laid siege to the house. They were incredibly quick and clever, ready to flash through any

opening. So flexible were their soft-boned bodies that
they could slip under the crack of an unsilled door.

It was on her second or third night in Panama that
Mamie was waked by a swish of wings and scrabble of
feet on the wall. She snapped on the light and saw a
furry shape flitting around the room.

She covered her head with the sheet and yelled, "Ike!
There's a bat in the room. Kill it!"

Ike rubbed his eyes and grinned. "I can't do that,
honey, it's against the law."

"Law or no law, you kill that bat!"

Ike knew an ultimatum when he heard one. He jumped
out of bed and looked for a weapon. His dress sword
was hanging on a hook. He drew it from its scabbard
and started in pursuit of the enemy. Mamie, peering
cautiously from under the bed clothes, saw her husband
in his pajamas racing around the room, making frantic
passes with the glittering blade, while the bat, darting
and swooping, evaded him with exquisite aerobatics.
She felt the cot shudder as Ike jumped on it. The sword
flashed in a tremendous lunge followed by a squeak and
a thud.

"Got him!" said Ike.

An officer's first duty is to care for the men under his
command. An officer's wife, as Mamie now fully realized,
has a similar duty to the wives and children of the
troops. The Twentieth Infantry was a Puerto Rican regiment with American officers. A great many of them were
accompanied by their wives, who increased the population with the carefree fecundity for which that island's
people are noted. It would probably be an exaggeration

to say that there were more children than troops at Camp Gaillard, but it would not be too far from the truth.

Conditions of life for the women and children were pretty primitive at best. At worst they were very nearly impossible. Due to the fact that Camp Gaillard was on the west bank of the Canal, while the railroad ran along the east side, and there were no bridges, all supplies had to be brought in by pack mules over the dirt road carved in the sheer sides of Culebra Cut. Every few weeks, with a roaring, quaking sound, a few acres of real estate would slide into the Canal in a confusion of trees, rocks, and clouds of dust, carrying the road with them. When this happened, the camp was cut off from food and other necessities, as well as from the hospitals at Ancon, sometimes for a whole week.

Then it was up to Mamie and the other officers' wives to see to it that the Puerto Rican women made the best use of their rations, and that small children somehow got enough canned milk to drink. The problem of caring for women in childbirth was acute. Mamie and other members of the Women's Club finally persuaded General Connor to lend them an abandoned house. They scrubbed and painted it, installed Army cots, and turned it into a makeshift hospital in charge of the chaplain's sister, who was a trained nurse. From that time on, the soldiers' babies were born there with modern care.

The ladies of the post also started a Sunday School where each of them taught in turn. At all times Mamie had to be ready to advise those of the soldiers' wives who were in trouble and to comfort the sick.

It is not surprising that she was good at her job, for, though she was still very young, her common sense and cheerful friendliness made her an able counselor. True, her advice often had to be given through an interpreter, for she knew no Spanish as yet, but the women, watching her with dark, worried eyes over a sick baby's cot or in the anxiety of domestic difficulties, felt her warmth and friendliness. They trusted her.

As for the children, tumbling around in flimsy clothes —or total lack of them, which the climate as well as poverty prescribed—Mamie loved them all. And they knew it.

At this time Mamie felt especially close to her regimental wards, for she was going to have another baby. She had known it back in December, but by that time Ike had accepted Fox Connor's offer and Mamie would not permit him to change. She had insisted on coming to Panama, for she would not allow her pregnancy to separate her from her husband or prevent her from taking her full share of the duties and difficulties of a tropical post.

Mamie's father and mother came to visit her that winter. Being such good sports, they thoroughly enjoyed life on the rim of the jungle, but Mrs. Doud put her foot down hard at the idea of Mamie's having her baby in such a primitive place. In April, when the rainy season set in and tropical downpours machine-gunned their sheet-iron roof while the jungle steamed like a Turkish bath, Mamie surrendered with a grin. "I do have a craving for some fresh Denver asparagus," she admitted.

John Sheldon Doud Eisenhower was born in Denver, on August 8, 1922. Just as soon as he was old enough to travel, he was indoctrinated into Army life. Mamie took him away from the comfortable house on Lafayette

Street and the doting Douds. With his bassinet, his condensed milk, his hamper full of diapers—disposable diapers had not been invented yet—and all multifarious impedimenta required for his health and happiness, they boarded an Army transport bound for Panama. She took a nurse from the Denver General Hospital with her. Made fearful by little Icky's death, Mamie kept this nurse until John was three and a half years old.

As the ship came alongside the dock at Cristobal, Mamie saw Ike grinning and waving. She thought he looked thinner in his fresh white uniform, and his face had lines she had never noticed. When he took off his cap to wave it, she looked squarely down on the crown of his head and observed that his hair was a lot thinner too.

Then she was carrying John down the steep gangway. Ike bounded halfway up it to hug her. He poked the baby in his half-shy, half-fearful man's way.

"Can I carry him?" he asked.

"You sure can," said Mamie.

The next two years were happy and fruitful for the Eisenhowers. Mamie settled down to the life as though she had been bred in the tropics. However, she never got used to the wonder and beauty of the brilliant scenery; the jungle, a vividly green ocean over which their hilltop house seemed to float like a captive balloon, the intense blue of the water, and the flamingo hues of a tropical sunrise. . . . It was like a child's painting in raw primary colors, and she took a childlike delight in it.

The days passed in a pleasant round of constructive activity. Although John took a lot of her time, Mamie did not skimp her obligations to the children of the camp. Marketing and housekeeping were difficult. She dared not buy any local food, but depended entirely on the post exchange. Nearly everything they ate was canned, though occasionally fresh lettuce and root vegetables came by ship from the States. There was, of course, no fresh milk. John was raised on Dryco, a powdered milk.

There was fun to be had, too. They often went to the ancient city of Panama, with its mellow sixteenth-century squares and the sea wall of great granite blocks which Don Alfonso Mercado de Villacorta had built in 1673 as a protection against piratically inclined British sea captains. America had brought sharp contrasts to the city. Opposite the great, age-yellowed cathedral the canopy of a movie theater advertised Rudolph Valentino in *The Shiek*. The narrow streets that passed between austere seventeenth-century Spanish houses, which were like forts with thick walls and small, barred windows, suddenly changed at no visible boundary into neat, grass-lined avenues with concrete sidewalks and unimaginative suburban bungalows in American-built Ancon.

To get to Panama City you had to drive up the dirt road to the Pedro Miguel Locks. The only way to cross the Canal was by walking over the broad gates of the locks. Then you took the train on the east bank. However, Ike invented a better system. With Mamie and several fellow officers he drove the Model-T Ford carefully out onto the steel grille of the lock gates. The two gates met in a very shallow V, which was too sharp an angle to turn. Ike drove the front wheels as far as he could onto the opposite gate. Then everybody got out and helped to lift the rear end of the car around. After that *tour de force*, they had motor transport to Panama City.

Mamie thoroughly enjoyed the horse shows in Panama

City, where the officers often exhibited their mounts. General Connor's Blacky was a great favorite. Otherwise there was very little outdoor life at Camp Gaillard because of the ferocious insects. When she went riding with Ike along the bosky jungle trails in the early morning, Mamie wore special thick-soled riding boots. Even on horseback you were not safe.

Their other amusements were the same as at any Army post—card parties, buffet suppers, and hops on Saturday night. The Connors were the Eisenhowers' closest friends. They had two daughters, Florence, aged eleven, and Betty, a grown-up nineteen. Since Mamie was nearer Betty's age than Mrs. Connor's, they became great friends. One of the great events of their last season was Betty's marriage.

An even more important occasion for the Eisenhowers was when General Connor was ordered to present Ike with the Distinguished Service Medal. The award was made with all military pomp on the Parade Ground at Gaillard. It seemed to Mamie that Connor was almost as happy to present the medal as Ike was to receive it.

In the winter of 1923 Mamie's sister Mike came to visit. At twenty she was still a tomboy, but a very attractive one with plenty of feminine charm. At dawn she rode with Ike and Mamie, and in the evening she flirted gaily with the bachelor officers.

Then one afternoon, Ike came home beaming with pleasure. "Swede Hazlett just turned up in a submarine," he said. "He's going to stay with us here."

"Who is Hazlett?" chorused Mamie and Mike.

"Lieutenant Commander Everett Hazlett to you all," said Ike. "He's the guy from Abilene who talked me into joining the Army."

"And I'm supposed to welcome him?" asked Mamie.

"If I hadn't joined the Army, you'd never have met me," Ike pointed out.

"Okay. We'll roll out a red carpet," Mamie agreed.

They were very gay while Swede was there. There were several parties at the Union Club in Panama, where they ate and danced in the soft out-of-doors on a terrace overlooking Panama Bay. They had picnics and other expeditions along the Canal. One day Swede took Ike for a dive in his submarine. Mamie was not too enthralled by that, but as usual she did not voice her anxiety.

Between times the two men had long discussions about the techniques of the two services and how they should supplement each other. On other evenings there were serious stag poker games—none of your "deuces wild" nonsense, but scientific draw poker. Hazlett records that they were a minor financial disaster for him. Apparently Mamie was quite correct in her evaluation of Ike's ability at cards.

When Swede sailed away in his narrow little craft and Mike went back to San Antonio, the Eisenhowers settled back to a routine that was mostly work.

Mamie had noticed the change in Ike when she came back from Denver. He was no longer discouraged or casual about his career. He had rigged up a workshop on the second-floor gallery of the house, and there he spent many evenings studying and planning, working out military problems on his large-scale maps.

His intense preoccupation with his work, Ike told Mamie, was due to Fox Connor's dark vision of the future, in which the general disagreed with most of his fellow countrymen. Those were the days of the great disarmament conferences, when all the principal naval powers agreed to limit the size of their fleets. Germany was prostrate and bankrupt in defeat; Russia was chaotic in the early stages of her sinister Marxian experiment; and Japan craftily appeared as eager for peace as the Western democracies. It seemed incredible to most Americans that there would be another war in their lifetimes—if ever.

General Connor thought differently. With a prophetic outlook, based on reason rather than occultism, he foresaw the rearmament of Germany, the resurgence of Russia, and the fantastic imperialistic ambitions of Japan. "If those three, or even two of them, unite against America," he told Eisenhower, "we shall not be fighting for ideals, as we did in the last war, but for our very lives."

Fox Connor believed that this terrible reversal of our seemingly secure position of 1923 would happen within fifteen or twenty years. He would be too old to be of any use in it, he said. It would be up to the younger men, to Ike's generation. "We will be disarmed and unready in our foolish way," he said. "Only men like you who have given your whole lives to military science can help us when that time comes."

Then he added with terrible urgency, "Make sure you are ready when America calls on you, for her need will be desperate."

One night they talked thus in Ike's veranda study until a red sun bounced over the jungled hills to fill the sky with crimson light. As Ike came down, Mamie, looking very touseled and pretty with sleep-heavy eyes, was bringing up John's six o'clock bottle.

"No wonder you get so tired," she said, "sitting up all night talking. It isn't worth it."

"It is worth more than getting tired," Ike said, and Mamie felt a sort of exaltation about him. "If Connor is right, it may be worth everything we believe in and love."

"Well, you can't get much sleep now. Come in and watch John have his bottle."

They stood together beside the cot, watching John suck powerfully on the nipple. He was going to be a big guy like his father, Mamie thought.

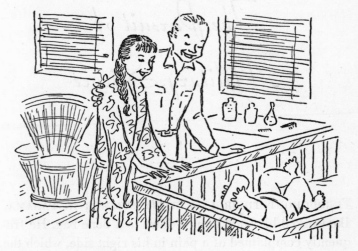

"I suppose he'll be ready for the Point before we know it," she said.

"Eighteen years," Ike muttered. "That may be just about it."

"What's it?" Mamie asked.

Ike grinned in a funny way. "Nothing," he said. "I'd better try to get a little rest."

17

The Pursuit of Military Science

THROUGHOUT THEIR LAST RAINY SUMMER IN PANAMA, Ike worked his body almost down to a bone bag. He frequently complained of a pain in his right side, which the doctors thought was chronic appendicitis. But he would not let up. He wanted to qualify for the General Staff School at Fort Leavenworth, which an officer must attend to be eligible for high command. Mamie did not interfere. She knew that Ike's consuming drive was not personal ambition but a sort of dedication.

In September, 1923, Ike was promoted to major, and his orders came for home. They arrived back at Camp Meade on October 1. Ike's new assignment must have seemed pretty silly to a man burning with an acolyte's zeal to serve his country: He was ordered to coach the Third Corps Area's football team!

Mamie went to all the games that Ike's (rather older) boys played, and she cheered conscientiously, though her heart was no longer in it, any more than was his.

However, Fox Connor was behind Ike, pulling every wire he could reach to get him the much-sought-after appointment to the General Staff School. He had become completely devoted to the Eisenhowers, not only because of his belief in Ike' abilities, but also because of his admiration for Mamie and the warm atmosphere of her home.

When the football season ended in Baltimore, Ike got orders to Fort Logan, Colorado, as recruiting officer. The explanation came in a letter from Panama:

> (Fort Logan) is a good place to mark time. Nice for Mamie to be with her folks. Meanwhile, *nil desperandum*.
>
> > *Fox Connor*

"He's such a thoughtful old dear," Mamie said when Ike showed her the letter. "I'd like to kiss him."

Accustomed as she was to vicissitudes of housing, Mamie gasped when she saw the cavern she was supposed to inhabit at Fort Logan. It was in the old officers' quarters, which had been built back when Denver was a mining town. The rooms were bare and enormous, with ceilings sixteen feet high. How to make a home out of that echoing mausoleum?

Luckily she had been accumulating more furniture. There was a fine old Sheraton dresser the Eisenhowers had saved for months to buy at Fort Meade. Mother

Eisenhower had sent Mamie a lovely old spool bed that
Ike's grandfather had taken across the plains when he
first moved to Kansas. Other things had been acquired
one at a time, always for cash, including the teapot and
cream pitcher of a silver service that Ike was buying for
her piece by piece. In addition there was some pretty
rattan furniture they had picked up in Panama.

Despite all Mamie's ingenuity the place still was
pretty forlorn. The furniture was lost under those towering ceilings. Then she had an inspiration. She had
bought some bright Japanese parasols in Panama. Now

she hung them upside down from the gaunt brass chandeliers. They gave the illusion of bringing the ceiling
down to a reasonable height. The apartment miracu-
lously seemed gay and cozy.

It *was* nice for Mamie to be near the Douds again.
Never had they been so close; for, as Ike and Mamie had
matured, there was no longer the sense of age-gap, that
most difficult barrier between parents and children. Ike

loved to tease his peppery mother-in-law, whom he now christened "Miss Min." Pooh Bah and Ike took up golf and often played together. On fine week ends they all went on picnics among the splendid red rocks of the foothills. The Douds usually insisted that two-year-old Johnny come, too. Mamie laughingly made the ancient complaint, indubitably invented by Neanderthal mothers, that his grandparents were "spoiling Johnny rotten."

Mamie's old friends took Ike to their hearts, and there were many small, pleasant parties, which the Eisenhowers returned by giving buffet suppers at their transformed apartment at Fort Logan.

It was all very gay and pleasant, but Mamie knew that under his surface contentment Ike was steaming. The urgency of his calling was upon him. He wrote for the problems used in other years at the General Staff School and studied them to tatters. As June boiled into July he felt he had to do something.

The first that Mamie knew about it was when she got a call from Fitzsimmons Hospital saying that Major Eisenhower had had his appendix out and was, in that irritating, hospital-worn phrase, "resting comfortably."

She tore down to the hospital. "What happened? Why wasn't I notified?"

Ike, still groggy from ether, muttered, "Didn't want to worry you, Honey. Thought I'd have it out when there was nothing doing. It might kick up sometime when I was real busy."

Ike recovered from the operation rapidly, but not from his discontent. Then one day, he rushed into their quarters, and pushed a telegram at Mamie:

BE READY. MAKE NO MOVE. DON'T EVEN BREATHE.

FOX CONNOR

On August 15, 1925, the Eisenhowers went to Leavenworth. It was wonderful to see Ike's radiant face. Also it was wonderfully and fearfully hot in Kansas.

This time Mamie drew a small, comparatively modern apartment in Otis Hall. She was lucky. A brick monstrosity across the way called the Beehive had over 100 apartments; Otis Hall had only 12. It was easy to get Johnny out to play in the safe, grassy yard. Her furniture, moved by the Army, was ample for the tiny rooms.

Best of all, the Johnny Walkers—he had been with Ike in the Fifty-seventh at Leon Springs—lived next door, and the Leonard Gerows—he was at Fort Sam the day they met—were across in the Beehive.

Fort Leavenworth was one of the Army's oldest posts, and therefore well appointed and gracious, with a beautiful Officers' Club. Its one drawback was that it was also the Alcatraz of the Army, where prisoners guilty of serious crimes were confined. Every once in a while a desperate man would break out of the forbidding cell blocks. Then the siren would shake the sky with its warning wails. Mamie and the other women would gather up their children and huddle together fearfully until the danger was past.

Despite such occasional alarms, life at Leavenworth offered many enjoyments. There were the usual buffet suppers. In such a close community, where any departure from the norm might be considered swank, Mamie found it better to stick to the unimaginative SOP (Standard Operating Procedure) of jellied veal loaf and tomato aspic salad, with a ham on the side. They made up for it at the big spreads at the Officers' Club where a fine turkey dinner with all the trimmings cost less than a dollar. On Saturday night there was always a gala club dance.

Such gaieties were a rare treat for Mamie; most of the time Ike was too busy to take her. She thought he had worked hard before, now he seemed absolutely possessed. The minute six o'clock supper was over, out came huge books and piles of papers. Often Mamie would wake up at one or two in the morning to find her husband still fighting his theoretical battles, while the mounds of cigarette stubs littered every ash tray.

At this point Ike got a remarkable demonstration of how the best war plans may be bolloxed up even in the middle of peace. He and Johnny Walker were serving on General Hanson Ely's staff. They were working out a theoretical problem, while one of those lurid Kansas thunderstorms added realism by simulating a bombardment. It suddenly became too real when a bolt of lightning struck a telephone wire over which someone was talking, knocking the general and his entire staff out cold.

In May, the pleasantest month in Kansas, Ike was no use to anybody. The final examinations were approaching and his absorption in his studies became demoniacal. Frequently he worked all night. All Mamie could do was to try to keep Johnny quiet, and force her husband to take ten minutes out to eat.

When examination time finally arrived, she was amazed that Ike was suddenly calm. He explained that he had done all he could, and there was no use worrying.

He was quite right. Pitted against the best brains in the Army in a course of such severity that many fine officers broke down under the strain, Eisenhower was graduated first in his class. It was not that he had the most brilliant mind or retentive memory; it was because the fierce compulsion of his new convictions drove him to do better than his best.

Of course, Mamie was not at all surprised. She expected such things of her Ike.

There was a fine celebration party given at the Muehlebach Hotel in Kansas City by Arthur Eisenhower, now an official of the Commerce Bank and Trust Company. Ike insisted on singing fifty-one verses of "Abdul the Bulbul Ameer." Then he went to Abilene for the first complete reunion of the Eisenhower brothers in 20 years, while Mamie went back to Leavenworth to pack for another move.

This time it was to Fort Benning, Georgia. Except for scrub pines and damp heat instead of prairies and aridity it was much like Fort Leavenworth—or Meade or Logan, for that matter. It was amazing how the Army could reduce any climate or terrain to a uniform pattern of mediocrity. Mamie began to think that the more she moved, the more it was the same thing.

However, the next shift was a real novelty for her. Ike's orders read:

> You will report to headquarters Battle Monuments Commission, Washington, D.C. for special duty preparing book, *A Guide to American Battlefields in Europe.*

Mamie had never expected that her husband would be ordered to write a book. Anything was possible in the Army.

In Washington, for the first time in her life, Mamie lived like a normal housewife. She found a big, old-fashioned apartment in the Wyoming Apartments at the corner of Connecticut Avenue and Columbia Road. It had three sunny, high-ceilinged bedrooms, a living room, dining room, and a large, antiquated kitchen, which she loved. Their furniture suited it beautifully except that the rattan pieces had to be replaced with real parlor furniture, which Pooh Bah helped her to get. The floors were brightened by a few good oriental rugs, which Ike was beginning to collect.

Mamie found life in Washington very pleasant. The Gerows were stationed there, and the Johnny Walkers lived in the same apartment as the Eisenhowers. Other Army friends made the apartment a center of gaiety. In addition, Ike's youngest brother, Milton, who had just graduated from Kansas State College, got a job with the Department of Agriculture, and was living in Washington with Sam Pickard, who had come from Kansas State to head the Department's new radio division. Milton was engaged to Helen Eakin of Kansas, who was also living with her family in Washington.

On July 1, 1927, Ike and Mamie celebrated their anniversary in their new apartment, and Ike had the tenth and last diamond set in her wedding ring, to which he had added a stone each year.

Mamie was not allowed to go to the next big party she gave at the Wyoming. She cooked the food, iced the champagne, and arranged the flowers. Then she retired meekly to her room. It was Milton's bachelor dinner, and, of course, strictly stag.

The next day, October 12, he was married. Ike was best man for his beloved brother, and Mamie thought he looked immoderately handsome in his dress blues, with the Distinguished Service medal on his broad chest, and his handsome, gold-hilted sword at his side. The sword served a traditional purpose: Helen and Milton used it to cut their wedding cake.

Meanwhile, Ike had finished the guide to the battlefields, on time, despite the vast, inchoate mass of material that the commission had dumped in his lap. Mamie was very proud of the letter that General John J. Pershing, who was head of the Battle Monuments Commission, wrote praising Ike's "superior ability" and "unusual intelligence."

From Battle Monuments Ike went on to the War College in Washington, where he completed his formal education in military science, though that was only the beginning of learning. He was graduated on June 20, 1928.

Mamie wondered with a sinking heart to what desolate spot his next orders would take them. It sank still further when Ike came in looking rather grumpy for him. "I have a choice of going on the General Staff here in Washington, or I can go back on the Battle Monuments Commission to revise the guide book. That would mean we have to go to Paris."

"Paris!" said Mamie, with sparkling eyes.

"I'm an Army officer, not a doggone Baedeker," Ike grumbled. "I want to be with troops."

"A free trip to Paris! Take it, Ike!"

"Do you really want it so much?"

"It would be very broadening for Johnny," Mamie said, and as Ike grinned, she added with something less than prescience, "We may never get another chance to go to Paris."

Ike thought it over. Mamie had never interfered with his career before, except about flying. She *had* been a good soldier. This was the least he could do for her; and maybe he'd learn something worthwhile on the old battlefields, which, if Fox Connor were right, might be the new ones of another war.

"Okay," he said. "Paris it is."

There were hearty congratulations and gay farewells. Only Johnny, who really was growing up, seemed depressed at the thought of leaving his best friends, who included Majors Gerow and Walker and Doctor Sam Beach.

Mamie had kept up the family practice of reading aloud to her son, and he had thus heard about the rites of blood brotherhood. Shortly before they left Washington, he came into the living room where Gerow, Walker, and Beach were talking with Ike and Mamie.

"I'd like you to be my blood brothers," he said solemnly to his friends. "Will you?"

"Why sure," they answered. "You show us how."

John trotted off, and came back with a darning needle and some iodine.

"We got to mix our blood," he explained.

Mamie intervened to sterilize the needle. Then she watched, half-proud, half-fearful, as John, with his small blond eyebrows knitted in a frown of intense, concentration, hacked away at his finger. She says that it seemed hours to her before a bright crimson drop appeared. The men each gravely took the needle in turn. Their blood was mingled with John's. After that they always wrote to him as Brother John.

Early in July the Eisenhowers sailed for Paris.

18

"Pont Mamie"

As would almost every woman in the world,
whether from Terre Haute on the Wabash or Muzaffara-
bad in the Vale of Kashmir, Mamie thrilled to Paris.
From the Gare St. Lazaire their cab, which Ike said he
suspected of being a veteran of the taxi army that won
the Battle of the Marne, zigzagged through the squawk-
ing melee of traffic on the Grands Boulevards and rocked
on squealing tires into the Rue de la Paix. The names on
the shops rang bells in Mamie's brain as would a roster
of battles in Ike's—Worth, Pacquin, Réboux, Coty,
Cartier. . . .

Around the Place Vendôme they swept, on to the col-
onnaded Rue de Rivoli, then across the Place de la Con-
corde, with the fountains playing and the old palaces
warm in the amber evening sunshine. The Champs

Élysées climbed between luxuriant horse chestnuts toward the splendid silhouette of the Arc de Triomphe against a golden sunset. It was so familiar, yet so wonderfully strange actually to be there, that Mamie felt as though she had walked through the frame into a lovely picture; emotion misted beauty in her eyes.

The practical business of finding a place to live, where a small boy would have room to play, with a school not too far away, soon superseded romantic estheticism. House hunting was easier for Mamie than for most newcomers, for when you are in the Army, there is no such thing as being a stranger in a strange land. The service is a small world that encompasses the globe, and there are always friends or friends of friends to welcome you and show you the ropes.

The wives of Ike's colleagues on the Battle Monuments Commission helped Mamie to find an ideal apartment on the Quai d'Auteuil, near where the Pont Mirabeau crosses the narrow Seine on three graceful arches. The building had a small grass court where John could play on the days when Mamie was too busy to take him to the Bois de Boulogne. A few blocks away, near the Trocadero, was the celebrated McJeanette School where, in September, John started his scholastic career at the age of six.

The apartment belonged to the Comtesse de Villefranche who had furnished it with Edwardian elegance: walls paneled in brocade; windows framed by satin draperies cinctured with ropes of twisted silk; exquisite Aubuisson carpets covering the floors; crystal chandeliers suspended from ornate ceilings; rooms crowded with gilt and brocade chairs, sofas and love seats; cabinets, escritoires, and innumerable small, fragile tables laden with Sèvres figurines, fans, and *bibelots*. Though the multiplicity of objects defeated the eye, everything there was first-rate of its kind, and the whole did have the beauty of style that the best of any period produces.

Seeing it, Mamie remembered the echoing empty cave into which she had moved at Fort Logan, and reflected that the distance between them was as far as Peary from Amundsen when they reached their respective poles. Yet in a few days, by a touch here, a picture there, she put the seal of her personality on it, and the apartment on the Quai d'Auteuil became a home.

It also became a center of informal hospitality for Army people in Paris—Captain Robert Schow, Harris

Jones, and Captain George Hoekan. The latter, in what
he thought was a fine burst of originality, christened it
Club Eisenhower! Almost inevitably the Pont Mirabeau
was renamed "Pont Mamie."

As soon as they were settled, Ike began his tours of
the battlefields. Mamie could not often go with him, because it was hard to leave John, but occasionally all
three of them made these excursions. Although she was,
if anything, over-conscious of the brilliance of her husband's mind, even Mamie was astonished by his knowledge of that bloodstained terrain. As they drove along
one of those straight white roads in country he had never
seen before, Ike would remark, "Now just over the next
rise there should be a small stream. The land is swampy
on this side and goes up in a V-shaped hill on the other.
The Forty-second Division lost 1,500 men taking that
hill." When they got there, Mamie would find that he
had described it with the accuracy of an eyewitness.

The three of them had a picnic lunch one day in the
somber, shattered forest of the Argonne. John listened
bug-eyed as his father described the last bitter fighting
of the war when American soldiers crawled forward
from tree to riven tree, almost like their ancestors in the
great American forests. Only instead of meeting arrows
or round bullets, they faced sudden machine-gun bursts
from behind fallen logs, the deadly blast of high ex-
plosives, and the stealthy death of poison gas.

On the way back to Paris they passed one of the great
military cemeteries. As he looked at the infinite perspec-
tive of ranked white crosses, Ike's face was grim. "Fox
Connor must be wrong," he said. "Men can't be that
crazy so soon again."

Mamie had been glad to come to Paris. In the hot summer of 1929, with the city boiling with American tourists spending the last dividends of the great boom and raising prices sky high, she was glad to be going home again. The one thing she regretted was that they would be unable to take a proposed trip to North Africa. Ike had been anxious to go because he believed that the southern shore of the Mediterranean might have a military significance that had been overlooked. Mamie thought that idea was pretty farfetched, but she would like to have seen the fabled Kasbah and compared the Atlas range to her beloved Rockies. She consoled herself with the thought that it was time they sent John to a good American public school. And it *would* be nice to settle down for a while, if possible.

Actually the next six and a half years, which she spent in Washington, were the nearest Mamie has ever come to settling down. Ike was made assistant to the Secretary of War on November 8, 1929. After serving in that capacity for nearly four years, General Douglas MacArthur, who was Chief of Staff, asked him to become his special assistant. Ike would have preferred a job in the field, but you do not argue with the Chief of Staff.

Mamie had sublet the apartment at the Wyoming, and so could get it back. It was like coming home. They picked up former ties and made many new ones. Milton and Helen were often with them. Among their closest new friends were the Harry Butchers.

The Eisenhowers had met the Butchers with Milton before they went to Paris. At that time Harry held a slightly anomalous position in the literary world as editor of *The Fertilizer Review*, published by the National Fertilizer Association. Now, through the interest of Milton's friend, Sam Pickard, he had become manager of the new Washington division of the Columbia Broadcasting Company. Butcher was born for the broadcasting business. He was as handsome as a movie star, with crisp, curly, golden hair, a classic profile, and smiling blue eyes. Unfair fate had filled that handsome head with an extremely agile mind—too agile it would seem later.

Ruth Butcher matched her husband well. She was a tall woman, tending toward the statuesque, with hair as gold and eyes as blue as handsome Harry's. Butcher's salary enabled her to dress superbly. Mamie considered them just about the most glamorous couple she knew. She still is very fond of Ruth.

The years Mamie spent in Washington brought radical changes to the United States and to the world, which had seemed so serene. They were the time of the great depression, when the rainbow bubble of false prosperity burst, and America slid from a peak of opulence unequaled in her history to the verge of bankruptcy. The economic structure of Europe was simultaneously affected, and riding on the resulting tumult a sinister figure came to great power for evil. The name of the man who thus profited by the almost universal misery was Adolf Hitler.

Though the Eisenhowers suffered little financially—Army pay, though small, is steady—Mamie was acutely conscious of the uncertainty of the times. In addition, retrenchment in congressional appropriations for the Army cut its size down still further, and made Ike's chances of advancement even slimmer. With her quite surprising financial good sense, Mamie economized rigidly in order to save for a darkening future.

19

A View of Corregidor

WHEN YOU STAY IN ONE PLACE, TIME SEEMS TO AC-
celerate. The years in Washington whizzed by, unmarked
by any major event in Mamie's life. Almost before she
knew it, John was in his last year at grade school, and
her one period of settled life was ending.

In September, 1935, Ike was confronted with a problem. And an opportunity.

General MacArthur, who had served nearly two terms
as Chief of Staff, had accepted the invitation of Presidente Manuel Quezon of the brand new Philippine Commonwealth to become Military Advisor to the Philippine
Army. Of course, there was no Philippine Army. The
process of giving the Islands their indepedence was just
beginning. MacArthur's task would be to build for the
new nation a military establishment capable of defend-
ing it against the menace of Japanese power, rapidly

becoming rampant in the Pacific. He needed a man he could trust, a man with the tact that would enable him to work with the proud, temperamental Filipinos and inspire them with ardor for their gigantic task. Above all, he needed a man with the technical knowledge and mental ability to help him draw up a feasible plan of defense. He asked Eisenhower to go with him.

It was a tremendous compliment, Ike told Mamie. Yet he was not happy. He ardently wanted to go to some regiment; he had been denied for so long the chance to be with troops. He talked it over with his wife to clear his own thinking, for she would not sway him. Opposed to his personal desires emerged a flagstaff-plain call of duty. The defense of the Philippines was essential to the safety of his country, since the Islands were the key to the whole southwestern Pacific. If he was needed there, and MacArthur insisted that he was, then there he must go. Ike was not conceited, but he was aware of his capabilities; he knew that he could do a good job. So he reluctantly accepted. His title was Assistant Military Advisor to the Commonwealth Government. In practice he became MacArthur's Chief of Staff.

After the decision was made, Mamie sadly told Ike that she could not go with him at first. "We've got to think of Johnnie," she said. "If he is yanked out of school, it may discombobulate him. He deserves to be allowed to graduate."

"You could not be more right," Ike agreed.

"We'll come the minute school is over."

"By golly, I'll be counting the days!" Ike said.

The original "slow boat to China" must have been an Army transport. It took Mamie and John 26 days to cross from San Francisco to Manila in July, 1935. Though monotonous, they were not unpleasant days. The ship ambled over the long, smooth rollers with hardly any motion at all except for the faint vibration of her engines. As each dawn revealed an identical circle of sky and placid sea, she seemed to be going nowhere and in no hurry to get there.

The voyage was broken when the transport docked at Pearl Harbor. Mamie had often heard it called "The Gibralter of the Pacific." The vast installations, the powerful, squat gray battleships neatly anchored in line, and the tiers of fortifications made it seem even more impregnable to her than the Rock of the Mediterranean.

Leaving Hawaii, the ship swam westward while the slow days lost their identity, and the heavy, wet warmth of the tropics pressed down on her passengers like an invisible blanket.

Mamie, as always, found congenial friends aboard, among them Major and Mrs. Arthur Nevins who had their children, a boy and a girl, with them. Mamie had known Art Nevins when he was with Ike at Leon Springs in the Fifty-ninth. He was on his way to rejoin that regiment, now stationed in the Philippines. Art and Ann Nevins were easy of manner and disposition, with vigorous, cultivated minds which made their companionship a never-failing delight. Mamie was afterward grateful that the voyage gave her time to know them well. Following the Shakespearean injunction, she "grappled them to her soul," and never let them go.

Manila Bay, at last, was as thrilling to John as to Mamie—to her because Ike was waiting there, while John, through his interest in military history, could picture Admiral Dewey's small, gray ships steaming silently up the channel past the Spanish forts. He stared intently at the humped Island of Corregidor, trying to imagine how it had looked that night when the action began with the Spanish guns twinkling like deadly fireflies from its embattled heights. Now it looked all green and peaceful, with no sign of its bristling defenses camouflaged by jungle growth or emplaced within the hewn rock galleries. Fort Drum on the other side of the channel was like a battleship of solid rock, with long twelve-inch rifled cannon mounted in a revolving turret.

The wide bay opened out, blue and serene, with ships drawing straight white tracks across it, and launches busy as water bugs. There was Cavite Naval Base with the slim gray masts of the Asiatic Squadron rising before the dry docks and warehouses. Soon their ship was edging up to a dock in Manila, and Mamie saw Ike standing there in his sparkling tropical whites. He looked just as young as he had that day in Panama when she carried John down the gangplank. Then he took off his cap to wave it, and she gasped in horror. His head glistened like the gold ball on a flagpole; there was no hair on it at all! Later she found that he had shaved it because of the heat.

In her bemusement Mamie almost, but not quite, failed to notice that the oak leaves on his shoulder straps had been transmuted by the potent alchemy of the War Department from the gold of a mere major to the silver of a lieutenant colonel. It was high time, she thought. Ike had been a major for thirteen years. She learned that his promotion had come on July 1, 1936, his twentieth wedding anniversary.

At first Mamie and Ike had a small apartment in the old part of the Manila Hotel, but as soon as the new air-conditioned wing was finished, they moved into a suite, which low prices and Ike's new rank made possible for them.

These quarters were definitely on the upward or palacial swing of Mamie's motley experience of housing. There was a big drawing room, which had walls lined with satin and a tremendous crystal chandelier. Fine oriental rugs covered the tiled floor; brocade and gilt furniture filled the room. "It was all very *"Louis Quinze,"* says Mamie. Ike said it was "too danged fancy to suit me."

Mamie's bedroom had tall windows looking across the docks, crowded with shipping, and the sparkling water of the bay to the green tadpole-shaped Island of Corregidor on the horizon rim. In the late afternoon she loved to lie on her bed, watching a tropical sunset light sky and water with the splendor of flamingo pink, lucent aquamarine, and the bright emerald of a parrot's wing.

There was another bedroom and bath for John when he was at home, though most of the time he was boarding at the Bishop Brent School in the cool hills at Baguio.

Since General MacArthur and Presidente Quezon were both in the United States and the new American High Commisisoner, Paul V. McNutt, had not yet arrived, Mamie had a little time to acclimatize herself to life in the Philippines before she was hurled into the social melee that characterized prewar Manila. But when the social season started, it went off quite literally with a bang she never forgot.

The occasion was a welcome-home dinner for the Presidente and General MacArthur, who had returned with his young bride. Ike and Mamie were dressing in their room. Suddenly Mamie felt a little dizzy; there was a roaring sound in her ears. "I feel queer, Ike," she said. "What is it?"

"It's not you, it's an earthquake," he answered. "By golly, it's a humdinger!"

The door of the room flew open. Through it Mamie could see the tiled floor of the drawing room rippling like a lake while the great chandelier swung in wild circles, its crystals splintering the light in fearfully beautiful patterns. Chairs and sofas marched up and down the heaving floor to the crashing accompaniment of breaking bric-a-brac. Plaster fell in clouds of white dust. Mamie was too stunned to be really frightened. Besides, Ike had a strong arm around her, so it was all right, whatever happened.

The shock lasted thirty seconds. There was never anything so quiet as the stillness that followed.

"It's all over," Ike said, grinning. "We'd better finish dressing."

Mamie managed a weak smile in return. "Does this always happen when Mac comes back?" she asked.

Manila was an important milestone in Mamie's life journey, for it was there that she first moved in the stratospheric realm of the upper echelons. The social system of Manila revolved around no less than three centers of power, each of them surrounded by guards, salutes, banners, bugle calls, and all the protocol of sovereignty. The American High Commissioner was top man, since the Philippines technically were not yet independent. During most of Mamie's stay in the Islands this post was held by Paul McNutt. A former Governor of Indiana, he was one of the most handsome men she ever had seen, with white curly hair above a youthful face, classic in modeling, enlivened by twinkling blue eyes. His wife, Kathleen McNutt, who became one of Mamie's favorite friends, was equally good-looking. Both the High Commissioner and his wife were naturally genial and gregarious people, but they had to keep up the formalities, because the Filipinos liked it that way, having oriental ideas about what was fitting and proper for their rulers. When the McNutts drove through Manila in their big open car, flying the High Commissioner's flag with its gold lion on a blue field above red and white stripes, delighted crowds usually gathered to cheer. However, if not enough people turned out, McNutt's Filipino chauffeur, who had a strong sense of the proprieties, would give the siren a whirl to attract attention. The McNutts could not stop him, though modest Kathleen always blushed in embarrassment.

In the Malecon Palace, Presidente Quezon, a thin flame of a man almost burned out by his passionate patriotism, lived in great splendor. Again this was not from choice, but because he believed that it was necessary for the dignity of his country.

The third center of power was MacArthur, who enhanced his enormous personal prestige with the Filipinos by his icy aloofness.

Jean MacArthur was as different as possible from her bridegroom. She was a friendly, dark-haired girl from Murfreesboro, Tennessee, whom the general had met when she was cruising around the world. With unexpected romanticism—which nevertheless seems to be characteristic of many a stern-browed soldier—he had pursued her to Murfreesboro, and married her.

Though her husband's preference for solitude kept
Jean at home most evenings, she loved the daytime hen
parties and had a warm and outgiving nature. Living in
the same hotel, she and Mamie became great friends. It
was an almost daily routine for them to rise early, as
everyone does in the tropics, and go window shopping—
if that phrase can be used where shops have no windows
—in the colorful bazaars of the old city, which displayed
everything a woman's heart desired, from French clothes
and perfumes to the exotic products of native craftsmen
in the remote islands. As the day warmed up, they might
drop in at the Army and Navy Club for a coke and some
refreshing gossip. Then home at noon to sleep out the
heat.

The formal parties came in the evening. There were
sometimes four or five in a night, and they were very
formal indeed. Manila was a rich city, with many luxurious homes, owned either by wealthy Filipinos or
members of the American colony. Among the latter were
numerous men who had come as troopers in the Spanish-
American War and remained to make their fortunes. The
city was self-consciously becoming a world capital, and
it preferred the etiquette of the old world to that of the
new. Everyone dressed in the height of fashion; medals
and decorations were worn by those who had them. Protocol was as strictly observed as in Dolly Madison's
White House. As a result, whether you were dining in
state with the Presidente or the High Commissioner, or
merely at one of the splendid private homes, you usually
sat next to the same person, because your place at the
table was exactly fixed by your rank.

For example, at Malecon Palace, Mrs. McNutt always
sat on the Presidente's right, and Mrs. MacArthur, if she

were there, on Quezon's left. Mamie often drew plump, smiling Vice-Presidente Sergio Osmeña and Weldon Jones, who had been Acting High Commissioner before McNutt arrived.

Such circumscribed gaieties and artificial manners were not to Mamie's taste or Ike's. But they were excellent training for her.

Luckily, life in the Philippines was not all white ties and tails. There were many evenings when the Eisenhowers could stay home and be friendly. Then the Nevins would come over from Fort McKinley for a bridge game; Captain and Mrs. Lucius Clay and other Army and civilian friends would drop in. After the game, they would all have dinner together in the hotel dining room, which was not a room at all, but an open pavilion with awnings that could be let down in the rainy season.

Occasionally, the Eisenhowers got away for a week end at Baguio, sixty miles inland, where Ike had set up the Philippine Military Academy to train the officers of the new Army in the West Point way. At Baguio they stayed at the spacious Officers' Club, and enjoyed the thrill of actually feeling *cold*, for Baguio, like Denver, was 5,000 feet high.

John could get out of school for the week ends. He and his father were great friends and companions. Even when he was a little boy, they used to have long, interesting conversations. Ike never evaded his son's childish questions in the foolish manner of many parents. No matter how queer or embarrassing they might be, John always got a straight, sensible, truthful answer. Now they talked completely on an adult plane, for John at fifteen, took an intelligent interest in all sorts of things, especially military science.

It was about this time that Ike took his son on an inspection trip to small Army posts in the far-off islands, where wild tribesmen lived in the untamed jungles just as they had before the Spaniards came.

On the Island of Cebu someone gave John a white cockatoo, which he insisted on bringing home with him despite Ike's protests. "Two things I hate, monkeys and cockatoos," he said. He would not stay in the same room with the bird, who was not really very satisfactory since it could only talk Morro.

The trip was a wonderful experience for John. After that he and Ike were closer than ever. But Mamie, secure in the knowledge that they would both rather be with her than anyone else, never felt shut out.

In addition to his other activities, Ike had taken up a new sport, flying. Mamie had at last consented because she realized that a knowledge of aeronautics had become an essential part of a military man's training. Also, Ike had been made responsible for organizing the embryo Philippine Air Corps. So this was necessary to his career and she would not stand in his way. But she was firmly resolved never to go up in a plane herself!

Every morning when he was in Manila, Ike would slip out of bed in the first glimmer of dawn and go off to Zablan Field for a flying lesson. He went in for flying with all the gusto of a teen-age boy. At dinner he could talk of nothing but planes, demonstrating the controls with a knife held between his legs like a joy stick.

Mamie hated every part of it. She would have been even more worried had she known that on Ike's first solo flight the controls had become partly jammed, and only his newly acquired skill, plus a lot of luck, had saved him from a crash. Ike kept that from her as he did every unpleasant thing that he could. When he won his pliot's license, he was so boyishly proud that she could not help but rejoice with him.

In addition to her worries about Ike's flying, Mamie was often lonely, for Ike was constantly on the go, organizing the training centers of the Philippine Army, inspiring officers and men with his impelling enthusiasm just as he had his football boys, and studying the terrain with an eye to defense. Even when in Manila he quite often got an invitation, which had the force of a royal command, to go off for a week end on the Presidential yacht, the *Casiana*. These parties were strictly stag, except for the Presidente's family. There were epic bridge games aboard, for Quezon was an expert, and Ike was his favorite partner.

Indeed, it may be said that though the Presidente had enormous respect for MacArthur and leaned heavily on his advice, Ike was the American he liked most, as Quezon was later to prove.

Meanwhile, Mamie's health was suffering from the climate. Her digestion and kidneys became affected, and she had to spend some time in the hospital at Baguio. Even when she returned to Manila, she was so weak and thin—she weighed less than a hundred pounds—that she had to spend long hours in bed watching the ships sail over the horizon toward America. Home was so incredibly far away—11,000 miles by slow steamer, which seemed farther than any place in the world does now. She became desperately homesick, but she never thought of going home until Ike got leave in the summer of 1938.

What fun it was for all of them to get back! Mamie had all but forgotten that it could be so wonderful just to breathe the crisp, clean air of Denver. She caught up on her old friendships, while Ike played golf with both John and Pooh Bah. He also had great fun driving the electric all over town at 12 miles per hour.

They made a short but pleasant visit to Ike's parents in Abilene. Then it was time to go back. Mamie hated the thought of it, but she was much refreshed. She knew that she could stick it out.

Back in Manila you could feel the tension rising every hour. Not that it was any less gay—they would still be dancing at the Manila Hotel when the Japanese were crashing through the suburbs. But there was nothing joyous about it. They had the feeling of looking over their shoulders at what was cryptically referred to as "the danger from the north."

The Japanese had begun the conquest of China in 1936, and as their armies plunged deeper into the Asian continent, they hardly bothered to conceal their imperialistic design for the domination of the whole Eastern world. The only question now was how many years, or days, or hours, MacArthur and Eisenhower and the valiant Filipinos had left in which to prepare.

In Europe, too, the lust for conquest was unmasked as Hitler's high-pitched voice rabble-roused his Nazis to the point of frenzy, and England and France helplessly accepted the inglorious truce of Munich.

American soldiers in the Islands were like men forewarned of a flood trying to strengthen a rickety levee with insufficient materials. They worked desperately, patching and improvising. They took breech-clouted

Morros from the hills, who had never seen a rifle, and made them into uniformed, disciplined soldiers in a month. It was a military miracle, but they all knew that it was not miraculous enough.

At the very peak of preparation, MacArthur received the second greatest blow of his life. He was ordered home!

For once his Olympian calm was shattered, his classic features distorted by emotion. "They can't do this," he stormed. "All I've worked for, all I've done will be lost!"

Then more calmly, like Caesar at the bridges of the Rubicon, "I shall not go!"

Nor did he. Presidente Quezon, feeling that MacArthur's departure would seal the doom of the Commonwealth, offered him supreme command of the Philippine Army. Unhesitatingly, MacArthur accepted. He resigned his four-star generalship in the United States Army, relinquishing all ties with the service to which he had devoted his whole life, to become Marshal of the Philippine Army.

Then, in the autumn of 1939, Ike was ordered home. It was another matter for him than it was for MacArthur. On September 1, Hitler's terrible armored columns had crossed the Polish frontier, while his screaming dive bombers destroyed the Polish Air Force between the dawn and dusk of a single day. The Nazis had conquered Poland in three weeks. England and France were at war with Germany. Fox Connor's words were coming terribly true.

Ike knew that his place was in America, though Presidente Quezon did not want to let him go. He and Osmeña begged Ike to accept almost any position he liked in the Philippine Army. When they found it was no use, Quezon said, "At least let me show my appreciation of the great services you have rendered my country. Let me present you with an annuity policy of one hundred thousand dollars."

Ike was almost struck dumb by this magnificent gesture. He shook his head, and then said, "Don't think I don't appreciate your great kindness, sir, but I can't accept."

"But I want to be sure that Mamie will always be provided for," Quezon said sincerely.

"Taking care of Mamie is my job," said Ike. "But I am most deeply touched, I'm overcome, by your thought."

The only thing Ike would accept was one small piece of metal, the Distinguished Service Cross of the Philippines. The Presidente awarded it at a splendid ceremony at the Malecon Palace. Mamie listened proudly as he made a speech in which appreciation of Ike's services was mingled with obvious affection.

When he had done the Presidente turned to Mamie, with his sad, sweet smile and handed her the glittering medal. "You pin it on," he said, "for you helped him to earn it."

There was a series of farewell parties, great formal dinners and simple buffet suppers. Filipinos and Americans hated to see the Eisenhowers go. The last tribute was the most surprising of all. Ike and Mamie were in their cabin, crowded with friends who had come to say good-by. A tall figure with the glittering gold embroidered cap of a Marshal of the Philippine Army loomed in the doorway, smiling across the cabin. Jean MacArthur followed him into the room. It was only the second time in history that MacArthur had ever come down to see someone off on a boat.

What is more, the MacArthurs stayed until the ship sailed. As it drew swiftly away from the dock and headed across the familiar bay toward home, the last thing Mamie saw was that tall, proud figure waving farewell, with tiny Jean clinging to his arm.

20

The Happy Things Happen at Fort Sam

IT WAS NOT QUITE AS WONDERFUL TO BE BACK IN AMERica as Mamie had hoped. For one thing those moving days began again. The Eisenhowers arrived in San Francisco on January 16, 1940. For two weeks, while Ike was on temporary duty at Headquarters Ninth Corps Area at the Presidio, Mamie lived in a small, drably furnished apartment in San Francisco. Then Ike was ordered, as Regimental Executive of the Fifteenth Infantry, to Fort Lewis in Washington State. So Mamie went back into regulation Army quarters. All her furniture, dusty and battered, was taken out of storage in Washington, D.C., and hauled across the continent. Routine set in. Things were just as they had always been.

But it seemed different to Mamie. During those years in the Philippines, especially the last months of growing tension, the Eisenhowers had lived with harsh reality, the danger of invasion pressing always upon them. They had forgotten how secure most Americans felt. Mamie found herself out of sympathy with people who talked casually of being able to "lick Japan in six months, if it comes to that."

She did not talk politics much herself, but Ike tried to explain the terrible dangers he foresaw in the Pacific. His civilian friends laughed, and nicknamed him "Alarmist Ike." That made Mamie boil.

Even Ike got discouraged and said he would resign from the Army, "if I wasn't sure they'd need me pretty soon."

He did not think much of his chances of promotion. At fifty, he was only a lieutenant colonel, which he had been temporarily over 20 years before. But he was philosophical about it. "Even though I never get much higher," he told Mamie and John, "I shall be content. There have been certain jobs to do and I believe I have done them well. I know I have the affection of my friends and the respect of the Army. I would not ask for more."

Mamie was content enough with that. And there were compensations to life at Fort Lewis. One of them was that Ike was so happy to be with troops again. The Fifteenth had been on duty in China. They were real veterans who lived up to the regimental motto, "Can do." Ike loved them.

Another pleasant thing was that Fort Lewis was only fifteen miles from Tacoma where Edgar Eisenhower had built up a prosperous law firm. Ike had hardly seen his brother since they each had been one half of a night fireman at the Belle Springs Creamery in Abilene. Now Edgar was at their quarters or they were at his house all the time. He took a tremendous liking to John, who at seventeen was a quiet, thoughtful boy, very thin and taller than his father. One evening Edgar startled Mamie and Ike by a generous proposal: If John would study law, his uncle would pay his way through college and take him into the firm. Since Edgar had no children, John would eventually have the whole lucrative practice.

John had been planning to go to West Point. But Mamie knew so well by now the hardships and frustrations of the Army that her heart leaped at this chance. It would give John everything a mother wants for her son. However, when Ike said, "That's magnificent Ed, but it's up to John," Mamie agreed, "John must decide."

So they called him in, and Edgar put forward his proposal. Just as Mamie knew he would, John said without hesitation, "I'm terribly grateful, Uncle Edgar, but I've decided to go to the Point—if they'll have me."

Mamie was both sorry and proud. These Eisenhower men were so darn idealistic!

John went off to Washington, D.C., to stay with Milton and Helen Eisenhower at Falls Church while he prepared for his examinations at Millard's prep school. Then, just as his father had, he went to Topeka, Kansas, to take the competitive examination for Senator Capper's appointment to the United States Military Academy. In the test he beat his father's old mark of 87.7 per cent, by scoring 92 per cent, the highest mark ever made in that examination in Kansas. Mamie nearly blew up with pride.

In May, 1940, the climate of American opinion

changed overnight. The Nazi armor smashed the "impregnable" Maginot Line at Sedan, broke the French Army and forced the British to flee across the sea, leaving all their equipment behind. In June France surrendered. With German troops holding most of Europe and staring hungrily across the Channel at beleaguered England, Americans suddenly felt naked of defense. People were panicky, and now Ike, since he had foreseen something like this, was no longer "alarmist," but much calmer than his civilian friends.

It was a new sensation to Mamie suddenly to become an authority on American defense just because she was married to a military man who had predicted danger. She was not an I-told-you-so type, so she simply soothed people by quoting Ike that America had time to make herself strong if everyone did their best.

Meanwhile, Congress had responded with billions of dollars to President Roosevelt's call for appropriations to strengthen our military establishment. The National Guard was called to the colors and a draft act was passed. Hundreds of thousands of men were pouring into the Army, while frantic preparations were made to train, equip, and house them. Regular Army officers worked from the first thin light of dawn until late at night and never finished. There was so much to be done. Mamie did not see much of her husband, whose regular working day was fourteen hours.

In November 20, 1940, Eisenhower was made Chief of Staff in the Headquarters of the Third Division at Fort Lewis.

As the Army expanded nearly ten times in the first full year of the new program, trained officers were at a premium. Even by March, 1941, many of Eisenhower's friends and classmates had been promoted, but he remained a lieutenant colonel. Early that month Ike was made Chief of Staff of the Ninth Army Corps, and on March 11, he received his promotion to full colonel (temporary).

Mamie and John, who would not start for West Point until June, staged quite a celebration that rainy evening when Ike pinned the eagles—"chickens" in Army slang —on his shoulder straps. Ike was jubilant; at last he had achieved the rank which for so long had been his goal. Many friends among the officers on the post dropped by to congratulate him. At least half of them said something about "a star on his shoulder soon."

Mamie could see that despite his jovial smile Ike was a little irked. When the family were finally alone he burst out, "I don't like all this talk about stars. Why can't they let a guy be happy with what he's got without taking all the joy out of it?"

Ike left Mamie at Fort Lewis while he went to California for maneuvers with the Ninth Corps. She knew he would do well in the great responsibilities of his new post. How well she had not realized, until in August, 1941, he was appointed Chief of Staff to Lieutenant General Walter Krueger, commanding the new Third Army. About a hundred colonels were eligible for that post, one of the most important a man of Eisenhower's rank could attain. Mamie felt that it showed surprisingly good sense on the part of those distant authorities in Washington to select Ike. She hurriedly began to pack. Headquarters of Third Army were at Fort Sam Houston.

That was one move that Mamie did not mind. Happy things had always happened at Fort Sam; the journey there was like coming home. It looked just as it had in those radiant days when Ike was courting her, and when she had come there as a bride. Only instead of a two-room apartment, she had one of the fine old brick houses, with shady verandas all around and a green putting lawn.

It was a big place, and she needed help to run it, so Ike, who was entitled to a striker, put up a notice on a bulletin board in the barracks and sent the applicants around to be interviewed by Mamie. That is how it happened that one day when she was doing the lunch dishes, very hot and tired, with soap on her hands and hair in her eyes, a spruce young soldier knocked at the back door. "I've come to see about being your striker, ma'am," he said.

Mamie looked at him hopefully. "What's your name?" she asked.

"Mickey, Ma'am."

"Mickey what?"

"Mickey McKeough, but everybody calls me Mickey."

"Are you regular Army?"

"No, Ma'am, but I've had fourteen weeks of intensive training."

With Army tradition behind her, fourteen weeks did not seem much to Mamie. "Do you know anything about being a striker?" she asked.

"No, Ma'am, but I've been a bellhop at the Hotel Plaza and I always helped my mother around the house."

He was such a cocky, friendly little fellow that Mamie took him. She made no mistake. His loyalty to Ike was touching and he became the first member of Eisenhower's official family.

Mickey went all the way with Ike from Fort Sam to

Berlin. When her husband left for the war, Mamie charged Mickey to take care of him. Later Mickey wrote to her from London: "I'm trying to keep the house clean for the General like you taught me to. . . ."

Mamie spent most of the late summer of 1941 alone, for Ike was with Third Army in Louisiana, where 900,-000 men were engaged in the greatest maneuvers ever held in peacetime. Their object was to try the quality of the new trainees and the ability of their commanders. Mamie knew that, as Krueger's Chief of Staff, Ike was largely responsible for the plans of Third Army in their mock battle with Lieutenant General Ben Lear's crack Second Army. On their success hung the reputation of the commanders and the proof of Ike's own career. Mamie did not worry about that at all; she had what might seem almost childlike faith in Ike's ability.

Her husband came home jubilant. He dashed into the house with his eyes sparkling and a grin as wide as a pie plate on his face. "We licked the pants off them," he told her. "If it had been a real war, Lear would have lost his whole danged army. Oh boy!"

Recognition was not long in coming; the mills of the Army grind a lot faster when war is close. On September 29, 1941, only two days after the maneuvers ended, Eisenhower was promoted to brigadier general. Mamie says, "That first star somehow meant more to us than all the other four."

In October she watched the review held in her husband's honor on the beautiful parade ground at Fort Sam, when Ike took his first salute as a general. To the spirited thump and boom of the bands, the long, ruler-straight lines of men, tipped with the flames of glittering

bayonets, legs moving, arms swinging in the precision
cadence of crack troops, swept by General Eisenhower,
who stood in front of a little group of officers. As each
platoon came abreast of him its officer hoarsely shouted,
"Eyes right!" and two long lines of heads snapped
around as one.

Mamie was not looking at the troops but at her husband. He appeared so stiff and soldierly, with his new
stars twinkling in the sunshine. As the colors came by, he
saluted with the snap of a West Pointer at his last parade. He seemed the essence of military virtue.

Yet Mamie knew that his stern aspect was a sham. Inside he was bursting with pride. There was something
so touching and boyish about the contradiction between
his martial manner and his inner self that her eyes grew
misty with love.

21

To Wait and Wonder

IN THE SUNSHINE OF SAN ANTONIO IT DID NOT SEEM POS-
sible to Mamie that things were as bad as the papers
said. Intellectually she was more aware of what was
happening than most American women, for Ike was there
to brief here on the significance of the ominous news. All
that summer she had followed the somber, dramatic
events: the Nazis' attack on Russia and their early sweeping victories; the Atlantic Charter Conference, when
Churchill and Roosevelt pledged their respective nations
to the defense of the Four Freedoms; the orders to American ships, guarding the convoys on which England's life
depended, to shoot on sight.

Then the focus of danger suddenly shifted to the
Far East. Implacable Tojo was made Premier of Japan
—dictator in effect. There were rumors of great Japanese troop concentrations in Southern China, of trans-

ports crowding the harbors of Formosa, so near the Philippines. Ike had said, "It won't be long now." And Mamie believed him.

And yet, on that springlike December Sunday at Fort Sam, danger seemed incredible and far away. Her mind recognized it, but refused to accept it. It was much more worrisome that Ike seemed so tired. His face looked drawn with the long days of work and worry. She begged him not to go to headquarters that morning. "You will do better for a day of rest," she said.

"I know," he answered. "But if we are going to West Point to see John at Christmas, I have to get as much done as possible."

That silenced her. She had not seen her son since June, and she wanted so much to go.

It was a lazy afternoon, with the Sunday papers to read while the warm wind blew through the open windows. Mamie was almost dozing when the telephone shrilled.

Ike's voice sounded harsh, as if he was giving orders on parade: "Well Mamie, it's come! The Japs are bombing Pearl Harbor!"

"Are you sure?" she gasped.

"Yes," barked Ike. "Turn on the radio. They know more than I do."

Even then it did not seem real. The excited voices of the newscasters gave her the sense of a bad dream. She remembered the great fortifications of Pearl Harbor and tried to picture the eruptions of flame and smoke, men dying and planes spouting fire, and great ships keeling over with their guns blazing as the scene was described before censorship clamped down. The sun was setting at Fort Sam. A single sharp report made Mamie jump. It was the sunset gun. The flag came slowly down while the bugles sounded sweetly.

It did not seem real to Mamie until December 12. At ten o'clock that morning, Ike came charging in the front door. Mamie's heart dropped into her stomach, but she managed a smile. "I see you've got your orders," she said. "Where are you going?"

"It's nothing much," Ike answered. "I'm called to Washington. They probably want advice about the Philippines. I'll only be gone a few days. Hey, Mickey, pack the small duffel bag!"

Mamie's heart climbed back to its proper place and slowed down. "Maybe they'll keep you in Washington," she said.

Ike almost glared at her. "That would be just my luck," he growled, "to sit out this war, too!"

They did keep Ike in Washington, first as Assistant Chief, War Plans Division, under his old friend Brigadier General Leonard Gerow, working on the "Pacific problem"; then, when Gerow was promoted to major general and sent to command the Twenty-ninth Division, Ike was made Assistant Chief of Staff in charge of War Plans. General George C. Marshall, Chief of Staff, who was "revitalizing" the high command, recognized ability without regard to rank.

Incidentally, Eisenhower was promoted to major general on March 27, 1942. It really seemed incidental to both him and Mamie. Sad news from Abilene had taken the joy out of Ike's second star. Father Eisenhower had died. He was a quiet man, but many people would miss him. Ike dared not leave Washington even long enough to go to the funeral.

Mamie waited at Fort Sam until she was sure that Ike was permanently settled in Washington. He was staying at the Milton Eisenhowers' house in Falls Church, and late in January Mamie joined him there. She stayed at Falls Church for a week while she went house hunting in war-jammed Washington. She was lucky enough to find a small but pleasant three-room apartment at the Wardman Park Hotel. They were there two months. On April 1, they moved into Ike's "permanent" quarters, one of the fine brick houses at Fort Myer. "That was April Fool for me all right," says Mamie.

In May Ike was sent to England on a mission of inspection and liason. Mamie had been bracing herself for the moment when he would go off to war. She was worried, of course, but it could have been so much worse. He would soon be back.

Ike returned late in the month. He told Mamie about the sights of wartime London, but never a word of what he had been doing. Nor did she want to know. She felt as strongly as her husband about officers who talked too much—even to their wives.

On the evening of June 15, 1942, Ike came home at the usual time. He was very casual—so casual, indeed, that Mamie knew something was up. She could not tell whether it was good or bad. Sometimes an unguarded expression in Ike's face showed high excitement, and once at dinner he looked as though he were seeing a million ghosts. When they were sitting in the parlor after dinner, he came out with it: "I'm going to London again —to stay."

So it was bad—for Mamie, anyway. She tried to be glad for Ike.

"What post are you going to have?" she asked.

Ike's voice was almost awe-stricken as he answered, "I'm going to command the whole shebang!"

There were many things to do and only a week to do them in. Ike was busy long hours at the War Department, going over plans and putting his personal staff together. He asked for Harry Butcher, who had resigned as vice president of Columbia Broadcasting to become a lieutenant commander in the Naval Reserve, as his naval aide. The Navy made a to-do about it—they wanted an Annapolis man in that key post. Ike stood firm. "I want one real friend with me," he told Mamie, "somebody who will tell me the truth, not yes me."

Meanwhile Mamie scurried around Washington buying the things Ike needed, or that she thought he needed. They usually met late at night in their quarters, but one afternoon she had him all to herself. Because of the rush, Ike had to take all at once the injections that are usually spread out over a week—typhus, tetanus, smallpox, typhoid. He got so sick he had to come home and go to bed. Mamie loved having him safely there in his room, even though she was careful not to bother him. He let off steam by reading a stack a foot high of his favorite "Westerns."

One Saturday John arrived from West Point for a week-end leave. Mamie knew it was the last time she would have her men home together for an unpredictably long time—perhaps ever. She made it as gay as possible, with a fine steak dinner and all their other favorite food. To blazes with rationing!

John had to go back Sunday afternoon. He hardly seemed to have arrived before the taxi was honking outside in the street to take him away again. They all went out on the front porch, gray-floored, white-columned, like the one at Fort Sam or any other fort. John picked his mother up and bear-hugged her till his two rows of brass buttons seemed printed on her body. He shook hands with Ike in an embarrassed, casual way. Then he marched down the straight gravel path.

Suddenly John stopped and about-faced as though he were on parade. For a second he stood facing his father, very tall and thin and solemn in the military splendor of his cadet gray. Then his hand snapped up to the visor of his cap in the full formality of the West Point salute.

It was one more thing than Mamie could bear. She burst into tears.

The years of Ike's absence and his great achievements were drab years for Mamie. On one thing she was determined: that was to remain in the background and not attempt to shine in Ike's reflected glory. That was the way, she felt, that she could help him most. There would not be any talk about her or any silly personal publicity, if she could help it. But it was not easy.

As soon as the news of his arrival in England broke, the reporters came down on Mamie like a pack of Assyrian wolves. Virtually nothing was known to the public about this Major General Eisenhower—he was soon made lieutenant general—who had been appointed to command the European Theater. A picture taken long ago with MacArthur and a reference in Hanson Baldwin's column in the New York *Times* about his achievements in the Louisiana maneuvers were all the personal publicity Ike had ever had. The public was avid for information.

Mamie, having had no experience whatever with the press, turned to Milton for help. Ike's brother set the attitude that Mamie and all the Eisenhowers followed throughout the war. "The American people are entitled to know what kind of a guy this is who is to command their sons in battle," he said. "So it's up to us to help them find out. We must see the reporters and give them all proper information about him. And keep ourselves in the background as much as possible."

Mamie loyally followed his advice. Her unaffected friendliness won most of the reporters. The regulars became, in fact, her friends, who respected her privacy as far as they were able, and interpreted her husband to their readers in the spirit of fairness. In that way Mamie helped Ike more than she knew.

His would-be biographers also came to her. With them she spent endless hours, digging in her memory for anecdotes; searching out old letters and papers; even giving small suppers so they could meet those of Ike's Army friends who were still in America. Nothing was too much trouble.

Meanwhile, Mamie's personal life was as quiet as she could make it. She moved back into the little apartment at the Wardman Park. "At least I knew where all the furniture went," she says. Ruth Butcher took an apartment across the hall. Since their husbands were together, they had much in common.

The company Mamie saw consisted mostly of Army wives whose husbands were serving with Ike. She had learned Mah Jong in the Philippines, and her greatest pleasure was playing it with these old friends; bridge seemed too exacting now.

Her health was quite poor. She had never completely recovered from the effects of three years in the tropics, and with Ike away the mainspring of her body seemed to have gone slack. It was then that she developed the trouble with her middle ear, which even now occasionally makes her liable to spells of dizziness. In addition, she felt a sort of claustrophobia, an unnatural, panicky wish to get away from crowds of people.

As Ike's responsibilities and reputation zoomed, Mamie was more and more in demand at the big Washington parties, which were a phenomenon of the era. She refused all of them except those to which she felt obligated to go for Ike's sake. When she did have to go, she was unhappily diffident. For example, early in 1945 she was asked by Mrs. Clarence Norton Goodwin to a large dinner party in honor of Vice-President and Mrs. Truman. That afternoon she called a couple who had worked with her on Ike's biography. "Are you going to Gussie Goodwin's?" she asked.

They said they were, and then the wife of the general whose brilliant victories had already made him the idol of the nation, asked shyly, "Do you mind if I tag along with you? I feel obliged to go, but those big parties terrify me when I'm alone."

Mrs. Goodwin was, in fact, one of the few people who succeeded in luring Mamie out of her shell. The dynamic, red-headed social leader from Chicago persuaded her to take a principal part in a project for strengthening the friendship between the peoples of the two Americas. At a time when our thoughts were fixed intently on events beyond our ocean moats, the necessity of hemispheric solidarity, though vital, was almost forgotten. Gussie Goodwin's way of rectifying this situation was to start a series of Spanish and Portuguese classes for the wives of high American officials, and English classes for the wives of Latin-American diplomats. The classes met at the homes of various members, and after the lectures the pupils had an informal lunch together, which they helped prepare themselves. The food was Spanish and the head cook was their Spanish teacher. Though he did not succeed in teaching them much Spanish, all agreed that his chicken *mole* was terrific.

Mamie was one of the founders of the Spanish Speaking Society, and signed the certificate of incorporation. In the casual atmosphere of people's kitchens she met not only the wives of most of the Latin American diplomats but of many of President Roosevelt's Cabinet and such important Washington women as Mesdames James Byrnes, Henry Wallace, Leverett Saltonstall, Robert Taft and Harry Truman. It was, in a sense, Mamie's intimate introduction to official Washington.

Mamie's other war work consisted in faithful attendance at servicemen's canteens in Washington. She took her full part, as far as her health allowed, but insisted on no publicity. In the main, she was just trying to keep going until Ike came home.

Meanwhile, there were his regular weekly letters— gay ones telling of pleasant trivial incidents about Butcher and Bedell Smith and Brad, and a lot about Telek, the Scottie his staff had given him; grave ones telling of his dearest hope of winning a real peace for mankind, of his soul-sickness of war.

Faithful Mickey wrote her too, filling in with homely details that made the strange far-off places seem close by and real.

Of course there were also exciting moments in her long tunnel of loneliness. One of them came in November, 1942. Washington was full of rumors that fall; something was plainly afoot in the ETO. Dispatches indicated that Ike was coming back for conferences with the combined Chiefs of Staff. Mamie believed them, and gaily prepared to welcome her husband home.

On November 6, Milton and Helen invited her to spend the night with them at Falls Church. They had a few friends in to talk and play cards. It was a pleasant evening, marred only by the fact that Milton insisted on keeping the radio going full blast. Mamie could not keep her mind on Mah Jong and more than once asked Milton, "Please turn that darn thing off."

Milton, who was usually the acme of consideration, became balky. He absolutely refused to do as he was asked, to the continued discomfort of his guests. Mamie tried to close her mind against the noise, but her head was aching. She had never known Milton to act so mean before. She soon found out that he had a good reason.

Suddenly there was an abrupt end to a jazzy number. Out of the grateful silence a voice spoke urgently: "We interrupt this program for an important announcement." Buzzing, clicks, and then the dramatic words: *"American and British troops under the command of Lieutenant General Dwight D. Eisenhower are landing at several points on the coast of North Africa."*

The best moment of all for Mamie came during the dark days when America was entering the third winter of the war. Ike—a four-star general now—had achieved great victories in North Africa and Sicily; but, except for a beachhead in Italy, Hitler's fortress of Europe was unbreached. It seemed impregnable, its beaches strewn with barbed wire and tank traps, enfiladed by Nazi cannon and machine guns; its interior defended by the tremendous German Army with its crack Panzer divisions, while the powerful Nazi Air Force still commanded its skies. No one dared guess what the cost in lives and matériel of reducing it would be. Or if it could be done at all. No one could even hope for the day when the war would end.

In December Mamie received word, a little ahead of the public announcements, that Ike had been appointed Supreme Commander of all the Allied forces gathering in England for the liberation of France. It was thrilling; it was awe-inspiring. She was filled with pride and joy for him. But she was not surprised, since she was loyally convinced that the remote hierachy of the President and the Prime Minister, their various cabinet ministers and the Combined Chiefs of Staff, who were lumped together in her mind as "they," had simply and sensibly picked the best man.

Then came news that touched her more closely. A general wearing the insignia of the General Staff came to her apartment. Even though the doors were closed and no one could possibly hear anything, he spoke in a whisper as he told Mamie that Ike would be coming back on a super-secret trip for conferences. He would arrive sometime in the night of January 1, 1944. It was the topmost of top secrets. No one must be told.

Mamie had a fanatic, almost a religious feeling toward security. You could not have pried her secret from her with hot pincers. She did not tell Ruth Butcher, whose husband was coming with Ike; or even John, who came to spend his Christmas leave with her. When she thought of Ike, she looked away from people lest they read the happiness in her eyes.

New Year's night was the longest she ever spent. By some excuse, she managed to keep Ruth Butcher home with her. They played Mah Jong; they played duplicate bridge; they listened to the radio. They talked interminably. Ruth wanted to go to bed, but Mamie plagued her to remain up.

At last her sharply attuned ears heard a scuffle in the back hall; a muffled laugh. The kitchen door flew open and Ike burst in, followed by Butch. Each man carried a tiny black Scottie puppy in his arms. The small sitting room turned into a subdued riot of laughter and yapping puppies, of love and happiness.

Of course the puppies—they were Telek's son and daughter—misbehaved and were shut up in a bathroom. Ike ransacked the iceboxes of both apartments for cold meat and raw onions. Then they sat and ate and talked until dawn.

The next two days, Sunday and Monday, went by in a blur of excitement. Sneaking in and out of back doors, rushed through the streets in curtained limousines, Ike hurried from place to place, for secret meetings—the White House, Quarters Number One at Fort Myer where General Marshall lived. Sometimes Mamie went with him. It was great fun, like playing a game of cops and robbers, but this was real.

On Monday night, they were spirited out of a back door of the Wardman Park into a car that took them to the shifting shadows of the railway yards. There they got aboard a private car on a special train that was to take the general to West Point to see his son. Mamie had never been in a private car before; but it seemed perfectly natural, as things do in a dream.

In the morning their car was on a siding in the station at West Point, under the sheer granite cliff on which the Academy is built. This concealed the car from curious eyes. On the other side the wintry river rushed by flecked with ice.

Ike was up early. He sent an aide up the cliff for John. The man was no more than out of sight than Ike began pacing up and down, glancing at his wrist watch, stooping to peer through the windows up the road cut in the side of the cliff. Mamie watched him with fond amusement. "It will take at least twenty minutes," she said.

"I know." Ike answered, and forced himself to sit down. In twenty seconds he bounced up and began pacing again.

John, dressed in dirty denims for the machine shop, came loping down the hill like a bighorn in the Rockies.

When he got near the car, Mamie saw him pull up sharply and walk on slowly. He came in breathless but seeming casual.

"Hi, Dad!"

"How goes it, John?"

They shook hands hard and quick. Mamie saw John's eyes light on the five-star circle on his father's shoulder. He kissed her. Then her two men sat down and began to talk—shop. John seemed so unconcerned he almost had his mother fooled. But, as she passed close by him, she saw that his hand was shaking. "So you *are* kind of excited," she whispered.

"I'm practically boiling," he whispered back.

The superintendent, Major General Francis B. Wilby, and his wife came to the car for lunch. Knowing what it would mean to John, Ike arranged with General Wilby for five of John's best friends to come for dinner. Then he sent his son up the hill to get him some of his favorite pajamas, which can only be bought at the cadet store.

John's five friends arrived for dinner in their dress uniforms. For secrecy they had been told they were to dine with General Wilby, and they had only just learned the truth. Their faces were bright red, their eyes blazing with excitement; but awe made them as stiff as the painted wooden soldiers they resembled. They were introduced as *Mister* Clarke, *Mister* Doolittle, and so forth. They sat rigidly on the edge of their chairs and quivered.

That was not Mamie's idea of a good party, so she went to work on the boys with all her might, ably seconded by Ike. Under that barrage of homespun charm you could literally see the cadets thaw. First they smiled and then they grinned, led by Mamie's deep infectious laughter and Ike's genial roar. By the time the steak came on that private car had become a Junior Club Eisenhower. When Mamie heard the cadets begin to advise the supreme commander on how to win the war, she knew her party was a success.

From West Point the Eisenhowers went back to Washington for a day, and then to White Sulphur Springs where the Greenbrier Hotel had been taken over as an Army hospital. For six precious days they were together there in a hotel cottage on a tree-clad hilltop. Ike made a flying trip to Kansas for a grand Eisenhower reunion, but he was gone less than 24 hours.

On Wednesday night, January 11, they boarded the special train for Washington. Mamie went home to the Wardman Park, while Ike lunched with General Marshall at the Pentagon. When he came back to the apartment, he had two hours before his plane took off for England.

Mamie does not like to remember those two hours. Up to now, she had been having a wonderful time, for she had the good sense and strength of character to keep her mind shut tight against the future and live for the happy present. Ike had found her as gay and radiant as when they rode the train from Denver to Abilene in the cloudless summer nearly 30 years ago. But with two hours left, Mamie could no longer shut her mind against reality.

They talked jerkily in brittle sentences. Mamie laughed, but for once it rang false like the stage laughter of a novice actress. She could almost feel him wishing it was over. Almost she, too, wished that the moment she dreaded would come quickly, before she lost the tight grip on her feelings that a soldier's wife must keep.

Mamie's self-control did not quite last out her ordeal. Just at the end she cracked. In the solid warmth of Ike's arms, weeping, she wailed, "Don't come back again till it's over, Ike. I can't stand losing you again."

22

The Shouting and the Tumult

As soon as possible after Ike left, Mamie went to San Antonio. It was not so lonely there. The Army let her use an apartment in the same bachelor officers' quarters where she and Ike had first set up housekeeping. Mike, married now to Lieutenant Colonel George Gordon Moore, who had been with Ike in Africa, had a pleasant home in town. Pooh Bah and Mamma Doud, who had sold the house on McCullough Street, were staying with her. It was a peaceful interlude.

In the spring Mamie went back to Washington, and early in June she and the Douds went to West Point to see John graduated. The ceremony was set for June 6, 1944. For a thousand years, or perhaps a hundred thousand, school children would memorize that date.

Mamie, sleeping in her room at the Hotel Thayer the night before, had no prevision of her husband standing taut with anxiety in the control tower of an English airfield, watching the planes carrying the One-hundred-first Airborne Division circle up the sky on their desperate mission of spearheading the landings in France; nor did she know that he paced through the night at his headquarters waiting for word from the half million British and American men sailing at his command through the black seas in rolling, plunging warships and transports and landing craft to storm the "impregnable" "Fortress of Europe."

They woke Mamie early to tell her that this was D day. She listened to radio flashes of news from the beaches of Normandy. Then, in a rebroadcast, she heard Ike's voice. It was strong and forceful, pounding his meaning clear with his sharp military enunciation. But knowing him so well, she could hear the overtones of deep emotion in his voice:

"Peoples of Western Europe! A landing was made this morning on the coast of France by troops of the Allied Expeditionary Force. . . . This landing is but the opening phase of the campaign in Western Europe. Great battles lie ahead. I call upon all who love freedom to stand with us. Keep your faith staunch! Our arms are resolute. Together we shall achieve victory!"

Despite the blur and crackle of the short-wave radio, Mamie could see him standing there, so earnest, so intense. When he ended, she seemed to see him take off his steel-rimmed spectacles and slowly fold them in their case. . . .

Mamie was so crammed with emotion—love, pride, yearning and fierce anxiety—that it would seem that her heart could take in no more. The sunny day passed dreamlike as she watched John go by in the perfect,

glittering lines of the last parade. Then in the dimness
of a groined and buttressed building she heard the young
male voices sing their farewell song; watched the cadet
caps fly, tumbling over and over, toward the ceiling as
the boys symbolically tossed away their youth and be-

came men; saw John, so straight and thin and solemn,
march up to take his diploma. These things, so moving
in themselves, were like a play she watched, not quite
real or touching her.

Yet there remained one more notch that emotion could
be stretched. That was the moment when Mamie pinned
the golden bars of a second lieutenant on John's new

uniform, and saw her son accoutered and ready to fight in his father's battles.

The summer was great with victory: France was liberated; the Nazi armies beaten back to their frontiers. Though Mamie rejoiced, she also worried, for Ike was always going down to the lines to see his boys. She told herself sharply that he was in so much less danger than the fighting troops she had no right to pamper herself by fear. To all her friends, even those closest to her, she seemed completely carefree. Nor did she let anything dim her capacity for laughter. She kept dread locked in a closet of her mind. But she could never forget it was there.

Everyone hoped for victory in the fall, but the German lines stiffened as they touched the Fatherland and the Allied troops bogged down in mud and shortages of supply. Then, coming as it always seemed to, in the gray winter days, disaster! The last desperate fling of Nazi power sent two great armored armies crashing through the American lines in the fog and rain of the Belgian forests. The Battle of the Bulge was the final terrible test of Eisenhower's generalship. In the first confusion and loss, there were voices crying of irreparable defeat. "Worse than Pearl Harbor," the unknowing said. Great victories were forgotten. Ike was to blame, the rumor mongers had it.

To all her anxious friends, Mamie appeared serene and confident. Oddly enough, that was how she felt, for she had a tremendous inner power to rise to an occasion. The criticisims of Ike did not worry her; they just made her mad. Her belief in him was so complete that she was totally unable to imagine his defeat. Not all the wild tales or even the true measure of danger, not grim von Runstedt and his long columns of tiger tanks blazing death from their swinging turrets, could shake her faith. It was, if you will, fond and foolish and feminine, but it was justified by what happened.

As everyone knows, a greater victory was snatched from the semblance of defeat. The last fresh Nazi armies were caught and crushed. With her power thus weakened, Germany became a setup for the final swift advance to end the war.

Mamie felt all along that Ike had planned it that way. Intellectually she came to know that this was not quite true—he told her that he had some bad moments at the Bulge. Nevertheless, she thinks that this is really just modesty on his part.

As Eisenhower's armies crashed through the reeling Nazi lines, came at last to the Rhine, spanned it, and went on to final victory, his prestige and popularity rose to heights unparalleled in the cynical twentieth century. We loved him, not for his deeds alone; but for his simple, homespun manner, his unmilitary friendliness, and his unaffected solicitude for his troops. To us, these qualities made him seem the archetypical American. Mamie did not realize how strong this feeling was; how exalted, her Ike's position. An incident that occurred in March, 1945, in the last days of Roosevelt's presidency, might have given her a clue to the future.

It happened that this biographer was conferring with Charles Michelson, who at that time headed public relations of the Democratic National Committee. Suddenly Michelson said, "What do you know about General Eisenhower's politics?"

"He has none, being an Army man," was the answer. "Why?"

"Because," Michelson said, "Roosevelt will never run again. We are going to have to have a darn good man to follow him, and we might need the general.

"Now," he added, very seriously. "We feel that Eisenhower should unofficially know that we are thinking about him. Will you see that he gets the message?"

Hatch hotfooted it up to the little apartment in the Wardman Park. Mamie was in bed with a slight cold, but looking completely charming in a ruffled bed jacket of her favorite pink, with a broad pink ribbon in her hair. After only the briefest greeting, Hatch burst out with his momentous message.

Mamie's reaction was utterly feminine. "Oh!" she gasped. And again, "Oh!" Then, as the implication sank in, *"Me in the White House!"*

Her lovely eyes sparked with wonder and excitement. "I'll put it on the teletype right away," said Mamie.

That message was almost undoubtedly Ike's first intimation of the presidency. He paid it no heed at all. Mamie soon forgot it. On sober reflection she was not so entranced by that glimmering vision.

The last tremendous months went by, and the drama of history spiraled to its crashing climax. In April President Roosevelt died. The free world was stunned and sorrowful, but events swept on. The armed might of Germany dissolved in chaos and death. Hitler shot himself in his bunker in Berlin, and his proud generals went to the red schoolhouse in Reims to beg Eisenhower for peace. They signed the unconditional surrender on May 7, 1945.

Throughout the war Mamie had been so amazingly successful in avoiding publicity that the American people hardly knew what she looked like. But the time was coming quickly when she could hide herself no longer.

The War Department announced that General Eisenhower would return for a brief visit on June 21, 1945. Immediately his admirers made plans for a welcome that would express all the relief of victory and their devotion to the man who had molded it. As the programs were arranged, Mamie alternated between joy at Ike's return and anxiety over the ordeal she must face. Her claustrophobic feeling in crowds was the main source of her fear. She did not worry for herself, but only that some weakness of hers might detract from Ike's triumph.

It is typical of Mamie's training in the unquestioning obedience of the military tradition, that she made no effort to influence the planning. Nor did anyone at the White House or Pentagon ask her preferences. She simply got her orders and obeyed them like a good soldier.

She did confide to a friend that she wished she had been offered some place on Pennsylvania Avenue where she could invite the Army wives, who had been close to her in the long lonely years, to watch the parade.

"Why don't you call up the President or General Marshall?" her confidant asked.

"I wouldn't do that for anything," Mamie said in horrified tones. "And don't you speak to anybody!"

Being an undisciplined civilian, her friend disobeyed her orders and told former Ambassador William Phillips about Mamie's problem. Phillips was horrified by the oversight and hurried to call it to the attention of Assistant Secretary of War John J. McCloy, who, equally appalled, arranged for windows for Mamie's guests near the White House.

Thursday, June 21, was a scorching day in Washington. Mamie got up early to dress in the costume she had chosen with a great deal of thought—it must be smart, but not too smart; becoming, but in no way flamboyant. It was a black faille suit with a rather full skirt. Around her neck was a double choker string of artificial pearls. She wore a small, perky, black hat with pink flowers, and a corsage of orchids.

An Army car came to take her to the airport with Mr. and Mrs. Doud and John, who had been given leave. There was a tremendous crowd, far more than had been expected, at the airport, and the military police holding the lines looked worried. Mamie was passed through the barriers and stood waiting with John, General Marshall, and the top brass.

At a little after eleven, the air began to quiver with distant motors. Mamie saw the glittering specks of fighters in the sky surrounding the long silver tube of the President's plane, the *Sacred Cow,* which was bringing Ike. Then the thirty-six fighters tore overhead at fifty feet, their snarling motors deafening thought. The *Sacred Cow* dropped out of formation and rolled up the runway.

Things happened fast. The landing platform was run up to the plane, the door swung open and, as Ike appeared, bedlam broke loose. Full-throated cheers roared, guns saluted, bands played unheard in the uproar. Then the crowd burst the thin line of soldiers, tossing Mamie, John, and General Marshall ahead of it like driftwood. Ike came down the steps and fought his way to them. He clasped Marshall's hand, grabbed Mamie and gave her a long hard kiss. "Gosh, Honey, you're looking great!"

Then Ike was swept away as MPs struggled to clear a path to the waiting command car. He and Marshall and John jumped into it. Eisenhower's party from the plane, which consisted of all ranks from General Bedell Smith to Sergeant Mickey McKeough, were bundled into the long line of cars waiting behind the general's, and off they went through a rolling barrage of cheers.

The next time Mamie saw Ike was from her seat in the visitors' gallery of the crowded House. Ike came in through a storm of cheers, which seemed as if it would never stop. Mamie was vastly proud of the speech he made; it was, she thought, a rare combination of common sense and idealism. The cheering was even louder when he finished.

The Douds and Mamie got caught in the crowd of congressmen and were twenty minutes late at the luncheon at the Statler. There she sat at a table close to the dais, where she could at least look up at Ike.

It was not until after the luncheon that she got close to him. In a long black car flying Ike's five-starred flag, they drove down the thunderous streets and through the great, wrought-iron gates of the White House. In the sudden quiet of the executive wing, President Truman greeted Mamie as an old friend and met Eisenhower for the first time. Then they all went out to the sunny rose garden, where the President pinned a second Distinguished Service medal with an oak-leaf cluster on Ike's uniform.

Ike said, "I'd rather have this medal than any distinction I know of."

Truman said emotionally, "I'd rather have it than be President."

Mamie knew he meant it.

The Eisenhowers were supposed to rest after that in the presidential suite at the Statler. Instead, Mamie sneaked Ike up to her little apartment at the Wardman Park, where a few old friends were asked to greet him. At seven-thirty they left for a big buffet supper at the White House. As she walked with Ike into the crowded East Room with its blazing chandeliers, Mamie suddenly found that she did not mind crowds at all so long as Ike was there. . . .

Because she would not fly, Mamie had to get up at four the next morning to catch a seven o'clock train to New York. Ike came on in the *Sacred Cow*. To reporters who met her at Pennsylvania Station Mamie simply said, "This is Ike's day. I have nothing to say on my own behalf."

So she kept in the background. From her seat near the platform at City Hall, she saw him come up Broadway in the blizzard of ticker tape and frenzied cheers. After the ceremonies they met for a moment in Mayor La Guardia's office. Mamie could not resist the chance of kidding Ike. She walked up to him and said impishly, "May I touch you?"

Then he was off again through the tumult, while she went to a luncheon given by Mrs. La Guardia, and then to the suite at the Waldorf to wait. The day ended with a great banquet. The next morning Mamie left by train for Kansas City, while Ike went to West Point and flew to Missouri the following day.

Through it all Mamie had succeeded in keeping very much in the background. Even in Kansas City the press featured Mother Eisenhower far more than she. The roaring welcome there was quite like New York's and Washington's, but at Abilene, where they went in a special train, Ike was just a hometown boy coming home. Mamie's heart warmed to the familiar Western voices and Ike's friends of long ago.

They stayed with Milton, who was now President of Kansas State College, for a day or two. Then back to Washington for a final ordeal of a state luncheon at the grandiose home of Secretary of War Henry L. Stimson.

After that came the time allotted for rest. The Eisenhowers went like homing pigeons to the little cottage among the trees at White Sulphur Springs. As she settled down alone with Ike at last, Mamie said with her usual lack of prescience, "It was wonderful, Ike, but thank goodness we'll never have to go through anything like that again!"

23

From Quarters One to Columbia

QUARTERS NUMBER ONE AT FORT MYER WERE THE EPIT-
ome of the Army house, its final exuberant flowering.
It had the familiar, dark red brick exterior, the white-
columned, gray-floored porches, the high-ceilinged
rooms, all on a Brobdingnagian scale. When Ike was
ordered home in November, 1945, to become Chief of
Staff of the United States Army, Mamie moved into this
pleasant monstrosity.

Downstairs, the house consisted of a whole suite of
spacious drawing rooms leading to a large dining room
for stately entertaining. Except when they had formal
guests, the Eisenhowers did not use them at all; it was
not Mamie's idea of a homelike place. They usually ate

in a breakfast nook off the dining room, and occasionally had tea or cocktails in a pleasant little library that seemed to have happened accidentally. Otherwise they lived entirely on the second floor.

The family living room was a large glassed-in sun porch filled with Mamie's rattan furniture brought from the Philippines. A billiard table took up a considerable part of the room; a movie projector and screen filled the rest. In the evening Ike liked to run a Wild West horse opera on it. If the film turned out to be a problem drama, he simply went to sleep.

Next to the sun porch was the room where Ike's trophies and decorations were displayed—the broad rainbow ribbons and medals sparkling with diamonds, bright silk banners, swords encrusted with jewels, and the placques presented to him by cities he had liberated. On one wall hung his commission as second lieutenant and next to it his commission as general of the Army.

Mamie liked to tag along when Ike showed someone through this room. It was fun to watch him—so boyishly proud of his trophies and gifts, just as pleased with each as though it were a surprise birthday present.

To help her run this big establishment, Mamie had three Negro sergeants. One of them, John Moany, became a permanent part of the family. Ike was also allowed a driver, Sergeant Leonard M. Dry, who had driven his jeep from the muddy lanes of Normandy to the concrete Autobahn that went to Berlin. Only Mickey was missing; he had retired from the Army to open a restaurant in New York.

At this time Rose Wood came to work for Mamie as her personal maid, and became the indispensable woman of the household.

Though Mamie had a good deal of help, running the Chief of Staff's menage was a big job. It seemed that virtually every great statesman and soldier of Europe who came to the United States wanted to see Ike in his home. In addition, a constant stream of politicians, industrialists, and other leaders of America sought introductions to him and were entertained at Quarters One. To them, as to her old friends, Mamie extended the hearty hospitality for which she soon became as well known in official and social circles as she had been in the Army.

This biographer was present when former British Ambassador Lord Halifax and his lady came for tea. The silver service, which Ike had bought for Mamie piece by piece, was brought in with a collation of thin bread and butter sandwiches, scones, and cakes. Just as Mamie was beginning to pour tea, General Eisenhower asked, "Would anybody rather have a drink?"

Lord Halifax looked tempted and said, "Well . . ."

"No you don't!" Mamie interrupted. "I went to all sorts of trouble to get the sort of tea Ike told me he used to have with you in England. Now you take your tea, and after that you can have a drink."

Halifax grinned, stuck his cigarette at a rakish angle in his black-gloved, artificial left hand, and drank his tea obediently.

Mamie's main worries at Quarters One were financial. Ike's salary was $15,500 a year, less tax; the house and the sergeants were free. Nevertheless, all those guests, whom Eisenhower's official position obliged him to entertain, ate and drank a costly quantity of provisions. It was only by extremely careful management that Mamie was able to stretch Ike's pay check, which he still handed over to her, to cover these contingencies.

Had she been married to a man of less integrity, Mamie would have had no such worries. Because of the demands of his position, the Army allots the Chief of Staff an additional $20,000 a year for entertaining. Though a good three-quarters of the people who poured through Quarters One were in reality guests of the nation, Ike would not draw against this special fund. "When I can't feed my friends on my salary, I'll quit," he said.

Only once in all his time as Chief of Staff did Ike put in a requisition for entertainment. That was when the State Department ordered him to give a huge party in honor of Field Marshal Viscount Montgomery of Alamein. Ike wanted to pay for the party for his old friend "Monty" himself, but it cost several thousand dollars and Mamie told him that he just did not have that much money.

All the Eisenhower brothers were brought together again in 1946 for the saddest reunion they ever had. Mother Eisenhower who had become very frail in the past few years died suddenly at the age of eighty-four. Mamie went with Ike to Abilene for the funeral service which was held in the little house on Fourth Street. Though she knew her husband needed all the comfort she could give him, she found it very hard to keep from breaking down; so strong was her own sorrow.

Except for that occasion the years at Fort Myer were serene and filled with pleasant happenings. In 1946 Mamie made a trip abroad with Ike—by ship. They stayed for a while in the twelve-room apartment at Culzean Castle above the Firth of Clyde, which had been given to Ike for life by the Scottish National Trust. John, on leave from the Army of Occupation in Austria, joined them there. All three Eisenhowers spent a week end at Balmoral with the King and Queen of England. Quite surprisingly, it was great fun. The royal residence turned out to be quite a simple country house, and King George and Queen Elizabeth (the mother of the present queen) were as pleasantly informal in their home as anybody in Denver. The first thing the queen said to Mamie was, "I hope you brought a hot water bottle."

When the Eisenhowers went there again in 1951 to lunch with Princess Elizabeth and the Duke of Edinburgh, the atmosphere was even more casual. Mamie

nearly stumbled over a wooden train, which the future queen kicked under the luncheon table, saying, "The children are always leaving their toys about."

Another happy event, which took place in 1947, was John's marriage. He met Barbara Thompson in Vienna, where her father, Colonel Percy Thompson, was stationed. When Mamie finally met Barbara at Quarters One shortly before the wedding, she instantly decided that if John had searched the world for a wife he could not have done better.

Barbara was a pretty brown-eyed girl with a round, smiling face. An "Army brat," she was wise in the ways of the service, and astonishingly innocent of the outside world. Indeed, she was more than a little frightened by the glare of publicity that beat upon the Eisenhowers. When the Army transport, which brought her home, anchored at Quarantine, reporters and photographers surrounded her eager to tell the American people what John's fiancée was like. Barbara's eyes were round with consternation. "What's this I'm getting into?" she asked. "I've always thought of John as just another Army officer."

She became worried at the prospect of meeting her almost legendary father-in-law-to-be; but ten minutes at Quarters One with Mamie and Ike dispelled that fear.

The simple wedding took place at Fort Monroe, Old Point Comfort, followed by a reception at the Officers' Club. Then the young couple went on to live as typical an Army life as they could manage under the circumstances. Naturally they were not entirely successful, but since they were completely in accord on the subject of keeping as far from the spotlight as possible, they managed to obtain a modicum of privacy—at least until the incredible year of 1952.

Ike's job as Chief of Staff was not altogether agreeable. He was obliged to preside over the too-rapid dissolution of the magnificent army that had gained his great victories. Not that he wanted to maintain an inordinate military establishment, but he was terribly concerned for the safety of America in the face of the rising tide of Russian aggression. Public impatience to get the boys out of uniform plus congressional economy stripped our defenses far more rapidly than was wise, as the Korean War was to prove. Tremendous political pressures were put on Ike to hurry things along. He resisted them with tact, understanding, and all the prestige that his secure place in the hearts of his countrymen gave him.

Many of the leading politicians became his friends— and Mamie's. At Quarters One she met such men as James Forrestal, the dedicated Secretary of Defense; Senator Arthur Vandenberg, whose wisdom brought about the bipartisan foreign policy; genial old Senator Tom Connally; John Snyder of the Treasury; John Steelman, President Truman's closest economic advisor; Steve Early whom she loved for his Irish wit; and Senator Henry Cabot Lodge, whose views on world affairs were closely meshed with Eisenhower's idealistic-realistic approach.

By the spring of 1947, Eisenhower had almost finished his particular job. Demobilization had been completed. A hard, efficient core of the Army had been saved, which could be expanded in time of peril. In addition, Ike's great dream of unification of the Army,

Navy, and Air Force in one Department of Defense seemed well on its way to realization under the able administration of Secretary Forrestal.

"It's about time I retired," Ike said to Mamie one evening. "I've done all I can here, and there is nowhere else for me to go in the Army, for it would embarrass one of my former subordinates to have me serving under him. Besides, I'd like to give Brad [General Omar Bradley] a crack at Chief of Staff. He deserves it, and he'd make a darn good one."

"Fine," said Mamie. "What do we plan to do?"

"I'd like to get a house in the country and go fishing," Ike said. Then he grinned. "But I don't feel that I'm about to stumble over my beard just yet, so I'd better try to find a job."

"You could probably be President if you wanted to," Mamie teased.

Ike exploded, "I don't!"

When word got around that Eisenhower was thinking of retiring from the Army, he got many offers. Several great corporations begged him to be their president or chairman of the board at $100,000 or more a year. He talked these offers over with Mamie.

"The way I feel is that I don't want to use the fame I gained serving my country for personal profit. All the same I could give you a lot of things you deserve. What do you think, Honey?"

"Just like you do, Ike," she answered. "We aren't going after money this late. Look some more, Ike!"

Then came an invitation to talk with two of the trustees of Columbia University. He met them in the same suite at the Thayer Hotel in West Point that Mamie had occupied on D day. When he got back to Quarters One, Mamie could see that he was pretty excited.

"They offered me the presidency of Columbia," he said.

"How do you feel about it?" she asked anxiously.

"It seems like a good idea," he said. "You know how much I want to work for the peace of the world and to influence young people. I think that Columbia is a place where I can make my ideas known without engaging in partisan politics."

"So you told them yes?" she asked with a sinking feeling.

"No," said Ike. "I told them that up to now our orders had always come from above, and you never had any say about what we were going to do. So this time you have to decide."

Mamie wanted to go to Columbia about as much as she wanted to live on Devil's Island. Her mind envisioned the continuing round of formal entertainments that a university president's wife must attend and give. She foresaw the goldfish-bowl sort of life it would be. In addition, she dreaded the crowds and hurry of New York, and the climate would be bad for her sinus and ear trouble. She also saw that Ike wanted very much to accept, and she thought it would be good for him.

"You've got to take it," she said. "It's just the ticket."

Mamie's quick decision did not fool Ike for a minute. He knew that she dreaded the move, and he would have refused it had he not been compelled by his feeling that at Columbia he could best continue to serve the American people. In print that statement has a too-good-to-be-true sound, but it is the stark truth—and Mamie knew it.

Ike tried to think of a way to make up to Mamie for

her sacrifice. He hit on the plan of giving her a really fine automobile. The first she knew about it was when Ike said, "Mamie, I've bought you a fine car, a Chrysler Imperial limousine, to get around New York in."

Mamie was radiant. "What a lovely present!"

Ike looked embarrassed. "The thing is," he muttered, "that though I put all my savings into it, I didn't have quite enough money. Could you lend me about a thousand dollars?"

"Sure can," said Mamie. Then they both roared with laughter.

Later, when they started for New York in the new car with Sergeant Dry at the wheel, Ike said, "Well, Mamie, we're riding to Columbia in our capital."

24

"The Groves of Academe"

THE PRESIDENT OF COLUMBIA'S HOUSE AT 60 MORNING-
side Drive was a Georgian style place of pink brick and
white marble about twice as big as Quarters One. It
had been built to the specifications of President Nicholas
Murray Butler, who enjoyed life in the grand manner.
The first floor consisted of a spacious entrance hall, a
long, elaborate drawing room, and a state dining room,
with a small reception room off it that Mamie used as the
family dining room. On the second floor was a suite of
slightly less formal rooms, including a big library and
a sitting hall. Third and fourth floors were bedroom
suites. The kitchen was in the basement. Mamie looked
the house over and decided that the kitchen would not
do at all.

Columbia's trustees were so delighted to get Eisenhower that they were ready to do anything to make

Mamie happy. Austere Thomas J. Watson, round, jovial Thomas Parkinson, and Marcellus Hartley Dodge, who was as spritely as a cricket and the most courteous man Mamie had ever known, all urged her to make suggestions. Then they had their architects draw up a plan of alterations, which they were told would cost Columbia $225,000. Slightly aghast, they consulted Ike and Mamie again.

It was sheer nonsense to spend money like that, the Eisenhowers agreed. Mamie insisted that the kitchen be brought upstairs for the convenience of the maids. This could be done by making the oversize dining room a few feet shorter. A kitchenette was installed on the bedroom floor where the Eisenhowers could—and did—cook their own meals when they felt like it. A sun porch was built on the flat roof of the house, where Mamie put the Philippine porch furniture. That is where the Eisenhowers spent most of their time.

Eisenhower retired as chief of staff in February, 1948. Mamie thought that they might have time for a short vacation before he took up his duties at Columbia, but that was not what happened. Instead, Ike took the two months' interim to record his own story of his campaigns for posterity. The writing of *Crusade in Europe* in so short a time was almost as stupendous a literary feat as the campaign was in a military way. The house was full of secretaries, editors from Doubleday who hoped to publish the book; and military aides running about checking facts. For eight hours every day Ike paced back and forth dictating steadily. At night they worked on revisions of the text. Mamie hardly saw her husband. It was worth it, though, for Eisenhower netted over $500,000 from the sale of the book. For the first time in their lives Ike and Mamie were financially secure.

Just as the book was finished, the Eisenhowers made a flying trip to see their first grandson, Dwight David Eisenhower II, who was born appropriately in the post hospital at West Point.

When the Chrysler turned into the driveway under the glass canopy at 60 Morningside after the long drive from Washington, John and Barbara were there to greet the Eisenhowers. Behind them was Mrs. C. Gage Lent, the housekeeper, and the three maids whom she had engaged to take care of the house. It was a sort of lord-of-the-manor welcome that amused both Ike and Mamie. Grandeur quickly evaporated when it was discovered that there was no food in the house. Since it was Sunday evening, the faculty club was closed, and nobody felt like going to a restaurant. In this emergency Mrs. Lent offered to run around to a delicatessen for some food. So that first evening the Eisenhowers picnicked on bologna and liverwurst in the solemn library.

Eisenhower was, of course, still general of the Army. He had explained to the university trustees that, if he were needed, his first duty was to the service: "I shall be in the Army as long as I am above ground!" For this reason the government allowed him two military aides, Lieutenant Colonel Craige Cannon and Major Robert Schulz, as well as Sergeants Moany and Dry. They were none too many, for during Eisenhower's term as president of Columbia he did almost as much work for the Army as for the university.

In fact, Ike never did get a chance to settle down to his job at Columbia. First there was the pressure of politics, which had begun back at Fort Myer. This consisted of intimations from both Republicans and Democrats that Ike could have the presidential nomination in 1948 by saying one word—yes.

Mamie, who had long since recovered from any notion that she wanted to be First Lady, viewed these overtures with apprehension. She knew that Ike did not want to be President, and would only accept if he were convinced that it was his duty thus to serve America. Mamie was scared that some of the silver-tongued politicians would be convincing. Craige Cannon and Bob Schulz, who were devoted to their general, were even more alarmed. "Don't let him do it," they jointly and severally begged. "He is so sensitive about his personal honor that the mud slinging of a political campaign would kill him."

Mamie did not feel that Ike was quite such a fragile flower, but she hoped he would refuse. And she said nothing.

The first crisis occurred when they were still at Quarters One. A National Draft Eisenhower League was formed, and Senator Charles W. Tobey of New Hampshire with Leonard V. Finder, publisher of the Manchester *Evening Leader* nominated him without his consent in the New Hampshire Republican primaries. That put it squarely up to Ike. He must either categorically refuse or, by silence, tacitly accept.

Only Mamie knew how hard was his choice. On the one hand was disinclination coupled with a tradition-rooted belief that a soldier should stay out of politics. On the other was the fact that so many people believed that he could unify the country and lead it in the way of world peace. He had such strong convictions about how this must be done and so passionate a belief in the overwhelming importance of American leadership of the free world that he wondered if he must accept the power to implement them. Most of all he was afraid that he might let personal preference tip the balance of judgment toward the easier course.

The letter he finally wrote to Finder categorically refusing the nomination sounded as though he had entertained no doubts. Mamie knew better. For six nights she had lain awake listening to the pad of Ike's bare feet as he paced up and down their room, wrestling with his soul.

Now at Columbia it all began again. Many Democrats by acclamation were convinced that President Truman could not be re-elected. In their despair they turned toward the man who everyone believed could carry either political party to victory. All through the spring there were increasing signs that Eisenhower might be nominated at the Democratic National Convention in July. Many prominent Democrats declared for him openly. Newspapermen quizzed him at every opportunity as to whether he would accept under such circumstances. Eisenhower said nothing. Knowing that Ike was a Republican in all but name—he had not, as yet, enrolled in the party—Mamie could not understand his silence.

Finally, on Sunday, July 4, 1948, a scant week before the convention, the situation was resolved. George Allen, the rotund and jolly "court jester" of the Truman administration, came to call at 60 Morningside. The Eisenhowers were fond of Allen and thought he had been maligned by the press. Mamie particularly enjoyed his impish wit, which constantly evoked her deep laugh.

This time George was not the least bit jolly. He had

come on a decidedly serious mission from President
Truman to ask Ike to declare again that he would under
no circumstances accept the Democratic nomination.

As they sat around in the sun porch, the air was thick
with tension. Allen kept needling Eisenhower to make
another statement. Ike maintained irascibly that what
he had said in January was plenty. Mamie had never
seen him so cross. Even the arrival of John and Barbara
with little David hardly erased the strain.

Then some friends came in with a copy of the New
York *Journal American* which carried a bright red head-
line: "IKE WILL ACCEPT."

That blew things wide open. "How dare they say
that?" Ike roared. "I've never even talked to them."

Allen read the article aloud, rolling out the words of
prediction meaningfully, while Ike snorted like a locomotive and Mamie wondered at the queer ways of
politics.

Allen finished reading. "Sort of proves my point," he
grinned.

"You're right," Eisenhower said angrily. "I'll have
to say something." Then he exploded his reason for silence: "I'm sure going to look like a darn fool, twice
refusing a crown that was not offered to me even once."

Eisenhower's statement that he "could not accept nomination for any political office" finally took him out of
politics—for good and all Mamie hoped. He played no
part in the campaign, though he did accept an invitation
to lunch with Governor Thomas E. Dewey, the Republican candidate, and gave him the benefit of his advice
about the military situation of the United States. This
was strictly nonpolitical.

Mamie thoroughly enjoyed that day at the governor's

farm in Pawling, New York. A mutual liking seemed to spring up instantly between the two men and between their wives. Tom Dewey, the alleged "city slicker," was as proud as a TOCH boy of his model farm, and the latent farmer in Ike responded. The Eisenhowers had such a good time that they yielded to the Deweys' hospitable invitation to stay on for a pick-up supper.

That fall Ike and Mamie registered for the first time, and voted for Tom Dewey.

Though Eisenhower had been acting as president of Columbia since June, he was not officially installed until October 12, 1948. It was one of the really great occasions of the academic world. The presidents of most of the American universities came, as well as distinguished scholars from all over the world. The Eisenhowers held a huge reception the night before in the rotunda of Low Memorial Library. Standing beside Ike in the receiving line, Mamie shook hands with over a thousand people. It was her first experience of mass receiving, and before it was through, her fingers felt so numb that she wondered if they would drop off.

In addition to the academicians, many of the Eisenhowers' friends came from all over the country. Ike's brothers, Arthur, Edgar, Earl, and Milton, held a sort of family reunion in Ike's office off the rotunda. When the receiving line finally broke up, Mamie and Ike joined them, and were in turn joined by such warm new friends as Mrs. Perle Mesta, Tom Watson, Harold Stassen, and the irrepressible George Allen. The latter evidently took a pessimistic view of his friend President Truman's chances of re-election, for he said loudly, "I'm sure going to enjoy this here inauguration tomorrow, because I have a feeling it's the last one I'll be going to for a long while."

There were more than 10,000 people seated on folding chairs in the great court of Columbia the following day. Every roof top and window ledge were black with swarming humanity. From her seat beside John in the front row Mamie watched the participants in stately academic procession wind two by two up the aisle to their seats on the platform. The gaily colored hoods on their black gowns proclaimed their degrees and the great universities they represented. In addition to the Americans there were scholars from Heidelberg and Salamanca, the Sorbonne, Oxford and Cambridge, and universities in China, India, and the rest of Europe and Asia and South America. Indeed, most of the nations of the world were represented in that galaxy of international learning.

Craning her neck, Mamie saw Ike walking alone at the tail of the procession, looking very solemn in his black scholastic robes. However, when he at last mounted the platform and took his place in a carved, thronelike chair, the inextinguishable Eisenhower grin broke out, and Mamie noted that Ike's mortar board had somehow achieved the rakish tilt of an overseas cap.

Then came the speeches, the presentation of the golden key of office, and Eisenhower's moving address. When it was over, Ike, preceded by the medieval mace bearer, paced slowly down the steps, followed the long procession. As the new president of Columbia reached the foot of the long flight of stairs, 10,000 people rose in unrehearsed homage.

Half crying, Mamie stood in the front row, watching Ike come slowly nearer. Suddenly, he did the most incredible thing a soldier could do. He slipped out of line, leaving the mace bearer in amazement and the procession in confusion. Mamie felt his arm around her, his lips on her cheek. Ike whispered, "Don't you ever stand up because of me, Mamie!"

Then he skipped back into line and, throwing the dignity of his position around him like a cloak, paced slowly on.

It must be recorded that Columbia was the least successful of Eisenhower's assignments, and that Mamie did not have her customary easy time winning friends there. There were many reasons for Ike's lack of success—mainly that he did not have enough time. Crises in the

Army kept recalling him to Washington; and the demands for speeches, to which he felt he must yield in order to make his views on world affairs as widely known as possible, took him all over the country.

In addition, there was an impenetrable core of opposition to Eisenhower among the faculty of Columbia. These professors had wanted a president chosen from their own ranks; they bitterly resented an outsider being put over them. That the "interloper" was also a military man, in their opinion, added insult to injury. The fact that he was generally more conservative in his thinking than they stamped him as "reactionary." They were determined not to like anything he did.

The faculty wives followed the opinion of their husbands—as good wives generally do. Except for certain individuals, Mamie simply could not break down their hostility. She offered them friendship and hospitality, and when they did not respond she let it go at that, devoting herself to such old friends as Ann Nevins, Kathleen McNutt, and Alice Snyder, whose husband, General Howard Mc. Snyder, was the Eisenhowers' trusted personal physician.

Of course, the Eisenhowers were also widely entertained by the most distinguished residents of New York, who were frankly charmed by Mamie's forthright manner and her responsiveness. These sophisticates thoroughly enjoyed going to Mamie's parties because of her unique ability to combine elegance with informality. In fact, outside the somewhat toxic Groves of Academe, Mamie was an unqualified success.

In the face of his difficulties Eisenhower did achieve some fine things at Columbia, among them the establishment of a Research Project on the Conservation of Human Resources; the Citizen Education Programs; the Center for Nutrition Research to help the hungry throughout the world; and the founding of the American Assembly, in which delegates representing every phase of American life and every shade of opinion—except communism—meet annually to discuss and air the complicated problems of our times.

Mamie and Ike also made some staunch friends in the academic world such as the Kevin McCanns—he is now president of Defiance College in Ohio—Professor Allen Nevins, brother of Art Nevins, Dean John Pegram, Physicist John Dunning, and Charles Glen King, the noted chemist and nutrition expert.

However, the Eisenhowers' greatest gain at Columbia was their own education. In a real sense, Mamie and Ike went to college for the first time in their lives, and they learned a lot—both from their widening contacts and from their own mistakes. Ike had never had the conventional military mind, but his opportunities for learning about civilian problems and ways of thinking obviously had been limited. He was avid to learn and, with the opportunities presented by his various contacts at Columbia and in New York, besides his travels around the country, his grasp of these things broadened immeasurably, as did his understanding of people.

Mamie went right along with him, and though she stubbed her toe with the faculty wives, she learned how not to do it again; while her increasing friendships, interests, and ease in the world beyond the Army's ramparts opened new vistas.

Indeed, the Eisenhowers, in the second year of their sojourn at Columbia, were at the turning point of real success when a tempest at the Pentagon ruined this prospect and almost wrecked Ike's heretofore robust health.

Eisenhower's cherished plan for the unification of the armed services in one Department of Defense had been made into law but not into fact. Interservice jealousy had sabotaged it, particularly the rivalry between the Navy and the Air Force. This had been patched up but not settled. Late in 1949 the Chief of Naval Operation, Admiral Louis Denfeld, suddenly tore the quarrel wide open by his acrid testimony before a congressional committee. There was only one man in America who had the confidence of the angry admirals, the intransigent airmen, and the anxious generals—one man with enough prestige to make them listen to reason. President Truman telephoned Eisenhower and asked him to act as mediator. Ike started for Washington on leave of absence from Columbia the next day.

Mamie spent the next two months in a parlor-and-bedroom at the Hotel Statler in Washington, trying to hold her husband together while he tried to keep the military establishment of the United States from coming apart. Never had Mamie seen Ike so completely upset. He saw the safety of America jeopardized by a foolish quarrel between the very men who were sworn to defend her, and it nearly killed him.

By enormous self-control he preserved his role of calm, genial, unbiased moderator at the day-long meetings. At night he walked sleeplessly up and down the hotel room, bursting out to Mamie all his despair and anguish. She listened and comforted him, soothing him with sensible comments or witty little jokes about the men who had lost their sense of humor. Then she would get up and make hot milk to ease the violent pains in his stomach.

In the end, reason prevailed. The Armed Services were brought to an agreement. It was the toughest victory Ike ever won—von Runstedt was never as bad. Mamie had a sick man on her hands.

General Synder diagnosed his illness as gastroenteritis brought on by overwork and nervous exhaustion. He ordered Ike to take three months' absolute rest and to give up smoking. This part of the cure was almost worse than the disease to the chain-smoking general. In fact, a year or so later when someone asked him if he was ever going to take up smoking again, he said, "I don't know about that, but I'll darn well never *give* it up again!"

The Eisenhowers went to a cottage at the Augusta National Golf Club in Georgia. There Mamie helped to cure her husband's nervous tension by presenting him with a set of oil paints and a blank canvas. Like Winston Churchill, Ike found complete and wonderful distraction in painting; he could lose himself for hours. Mamie encouraged him and praised his work extravagantly. In truth, it was remarkably good, with something in it of the primitive starkness of the itinerant portrait painters of eighteenth-century America.

By May, 1950, the Eisenhowers were back at Columbia. Ike, completely restored, plunged into his work with tremendous vigor. In June the Korean War began. Again Washington called for help, and Ike began commuting between jobs.

Despite all this, it was a fairly peaceful summer, enlivened by a trip to Denver and a return visit from the Douds. Mamie was terribly worried about Pooh Bah, who was failing visibly.

Both Mamie and Ike had always wanted to own a

home. Now they bought a good-sized farm at Gettysburg, remembering how happy they had been there. The old brick house had been right between the armies on those terrible July days of 1863, but it had come through unscathed. Mamie had a wonderful time planning how to fix it up. She looked forward to the day when Ike would retire and they could live there in peace.

In the autumn they again had the illusion of being settled at Columbia. However, Mamie kept her fingers crossed. A lot of politicians came calling—Senator Lodge, and bluff old Senator James H. Duff of Pennsylvania, Roy Roberts of the Kansas City *Star*, Governor Dewey and many more. This meant the presidential pressure was being turned on again. Mamie learned that they felt that in 1952 the Republicans had to have a winner or perish. She knew that Ike was greatly troubled by the course the Democratic administration was taking—not only in Far Eastern affairs, but in their slow drift toward a welfare state.

"What about it, Ike?" she once asked. "Are you going to take it?"

"I don't know," he replied. "Mebbe I'll have to."

As it turned out, Eisenhower did not have to make up his mind just then about the Presidency or anything else. It was made up for him by world events that abruptly changed the course of his life, and started Mamie moving again.

25

The Shape of Things

THE NORTH ATLANTIC TREATY ORGANIZATION, WHICH came into effect in 1949, was designed to defend western Europe from the threat of Communist imperialism. A Supreme Commander was to be appointed for the joint forces of the twelve member nations. Again it seemed that Eisenhower was the best man, the only one whom everybody trusted. In December, 1950, President Truman offered him the job. This time Mamie was not consulted—it was a clear call of duty. Ike accepted, though reluctantly.

As soon as word came from Washington, Mamie began to pack. There was an immense amount to be done. The Eisenhowers' personal possessions had to be separated from the Columbia furnishings and sent to storage, or so Mamie felt.

"Why go to all this trouble?" a friend asked her.

"You could leave the stuff here. The General is only on leave from Columbia; surely you will be coming back when his assignment is over."

In a completely matter-of-fact tone Mamie answered, "Sure we'll come back if we can; but even in western Europe there are about twenty million Communists, and every one of them will be out to get Ike. You just can't be sure."

General Eisenhower assumed command of the NATO forces in January, 1951. Being somewhat superstitious about names, he called it SHAPE (Supreme Headquarters Allied Powers in Europe), which echoed the sound of his lucky wartime headquarters, SHAEF. After setting up the organization, he flew home to fetch Mamie.

Early in February the Eisenhowers left for France by ship; Mamie still would not fly. With them went their faithful official family, General and Mrs. Snyder, Rose, and Sergeants Dry and Moany. Bob Schulz, now a lieutenant colonel, had gone on ahead.

The Eisenhowers went straight to Versailles. Ike had picked out a pleasant modern apartment at the Hotel Trianon, where he had lived during the final phase of his great campaign. Mamie liked his choice, though the French were prudently economical with the heat. When Mamie plugged in an American electric heater, it blew out every fuse in the place. The leftist French press, which was gunning for Eisenhower, made a great to-do about the incident. Mamie had burnt her fingers, so to speak, on a heater that wouldn't work.

Although Mamie liked the apartment, she was not allowed to keep it, since it was not large enough for the entertaining the Supreme Commander must do. So she went house hunting and again fell afoul of the French newspapers.

For their official residence the French government offered the Eisenhowers a huge villa formerly owned by society-minded Lady Mendl, whose avocation was interior decorating. When Mamie saw the house, it looked like Messrs. Metro, Goldwyn and Mayers' dream of high life in the International Set. You might, perhaps, *reside* in its ornate grandeurs, but you could not possibly *live* there. She turned it down.

Whereupon the whole French press jumped on her. Who did this American general's wife think she was, refusing the generous offer of the French government? Who was she to set herself up as an arbiter of good taste and criticize the artistic judgment of a people famous for their flair? Her refusal, it seemed, was a personal insult to the entire French nation. (Lady Mendl had been an American.)

What Mamie was looking for was some place where she could make a home for Ike. The last thing she had intended was to insult anybody. The thought that she had tarnished Ike's popularity and made his task more difficult made her so unhappy that she cried all over the front page of *Le Matin*.

Then she got good and mad. All her married life she had lived in other people's houses, but at least she had been allowed to do what she could with them. If her taste clashed with the famous *goût français*, it was just too bad. She would rather stay in the apartment at the Hotel Trianon anyhow.

At this point the harassed French officials suggested that she look at the Villa St. Pierre at Marnes La Coquette, ten miles west of Paris and only a few minutes' drive from the miniature Pentagon the French Government was building in the national forest of Marly to house SHAPE. To their profuse relief, Mamie said it was perfect.

The Villa St. Pierre was a charming country house set on a small knoll with lawns sloping down to a little artificial lake. It had simple, classic Regency lines and, though it seemed small, the interior was quite spacious, with long French windows overlooking turf that stayed green all winter. Mamie knew that she and Ike could be happy there, but first she had to furnish it livably. There was a little difficulty about that.

The French government was as courteously anxious to please as Columbia's trustees had been. They put the precious antiques from a national museum at Mamie's disposal. They also sent a staff of eight famous Parisian decorators down to help her. That was where the trouble began again.

Mamie proposed to use the lovely old pieces from the museum to furnish her new home in the classic style consonent with its architecture. The decorators saw in it a wonderful display case for their wares and an opportunity to show what they could do in the line of modern decoration. The resulting clash was sharpened by the fact that all eight knew only a few English words between them, and Mamie's French was rudimentary.

In the end, the Battle of Marnes La Coquette was just about a draw. Mamie succeeded in keeping the main effect simple and traditional, but she lost several skirmishes. When she wasn't looking, the decorators installed modernistic, office-type lighting fixtures in the dining room. The magazine rack in the sitting room looked slightly like a newsstand in Grand Central Station. There was a little alcove separated from the drawing room by fluted columns. Mamie thought it would be a cozy place to play cards, and suggested an overhead light. She got a chandelier that would have looked fine

A. G.

in the East Room of the White House. All the pictures belonged to the modern school of art, which she hated. Overcompensating, perhaps, in her pleasant yellow and green bedroom, Mamie hung a landscape her husband had copied in oils from an English calendar.

The final touch came when Mamie suggested that she would like a simple, wrought-iron, glass-topped table for the second-floor sitting room, where she and Ike could eat when they were alone. Six sweating men staggered up the stairs with a huge circular slab of green marble poised on an amazing curlicue base. When Mamie showed it to Eileen Archibold, who was over from Denver on a visit, she added plaintively, "I wish I had paid a little more attention to my French at Miss Wolcott's."

Despite the trials and errors attendant on her twenty-eighth move, Mamie loved the Villa St. Pierre. Reminiscing about it, she spoke nostalgically of the view from her bedroom window. "It was so serene. The lawns and fields had so many shades of green. There were stately old trees. I could see the lovely little pond with its Japanese bridge. I loved that bridge. Something was always going on: a cat would walk over it; birds perched on the railings; a fish would jump in the pond. . . ."

She had a putting green made for Ike and had the pond stocked with trout. When unexpected guests came for dinner, she would send Moany out to catch some fish, and would direct his efforts from her window: "Better catch a couple more. We don't want to seem skimpy."

In the nearby forest of Marly the cuckoos called all night long. It was the first time Mamie had heard them —"I always thought they were a mythical bird that only came in clocks."

The great worlds of diplomacy, war, and politics poured through the Villa St. Pierre. Mamie gave many stately parties for them with the exquisite food and vintage wines they all loved. But even in Europe she managed to alleviate protocol with a sense of humor.

When the Eisenhowers dined alone or with fellow Americans, Ike got the kind of food he liked—roast beef, onions, and home-baked beans. In summer there was corn on the cob, which Mamie succeeded in growing in the unsuitable climate of France by planting it against a wall with a southern exposure.

Mamie needed the happiness and serenity of this pleasant house; for she came to it after a blow that she had dreaded throughout the past few years. While she was still at the Hotel Trianon, Mrs. Doud came over to visit her. Shortly after her arrival came the news that their beloved Pooh Bah had died of a heart attack in Denver.

Mrs. Doud determined to fly home immediately, and Mamie's sorrow for her father and anxiety for Mamma Doud overcame her fear of flying. The Supreme Commander's Air Force Constellation was put at their disposal. In it Mamie and her mother flew directly to Denver. A stormy Atlantic crossing was hardly a soothing voyage for a beginner, but Mamie felt that it was the right thing to do, and so she did it. Her one concession to nervousness was to say to the General's pilot, Lieutenant-Colonel William G. Draper, "Please fly nice and low."

From that time on Mamie has flown almost everywhere with Ike. In the summer of 1951 she went with him on official visits to many of the NATO countries, including Sweden, Norway, Denmark, England, and Holland. On a trip to Luxembourg they stayed with their friend Perle Mesta, who was having as wonderful a time as minister to that musical-comedy country as her prototype, Ethel Merman, did in *Call Me Madam*. In Holland Mamie found a fellow canasta enthusiast in Queen Juliana.

In the course of these travels Mamie became quite casually accustomed to staying with kings and queens and amusing prime ministers with dinner table chit-chat.

She also got used to flying, and, in fact, became so fond
of General Eisenhower's luxurious Constellation, which
had been built and equipped by the Air Force especially
for transporting VIPs, that she suggested naming it *The
Columbine* after the state flower of Colorado.

Though Mamie had been sure that Ike's appointment
to SHAPE had laid that business of the presidency permanently to rest; she soon learned that it was only in
abeyance. By July, 1951, the politicians began dropping
in at Marnes La Coquette for significant little chats with
Ike. Mamie already knew some of them like Lodge and
Duff. She met many others for the first time. One of her
favorites was Senator Frank Carlson of Kansas, who
looked like a kind, shaggy bear. Carlson was transparently honest and straightforward, very gentle and wise.
He spoke in the nice, familiar accent of the Midwest.
Mamie instinctively trusted him and was ready to believe that whatever he said was the right thing to do.

Another man, whom Mamie liked immensely, had
great weight in Eisenhower's final decision. This was
William Robinson, Executive Vice-President of the New
York *Herald Tribune*. Bill Robinson, though an ardent
Republican, was not interested in any political office. He
had no ax to grind, and was interested solely in what he
believed to be the best interests of the United States.

Mamie, who was beginning to learn about politics,
knew that all these men were urging Ike to run for the
Republican nomination. He was, they said, the only man
strong enough to give the Republican Party progressive
leadership and assure victory in the next election. This
time there would be no silver platter present of the nomination. Ike would have to fight for it against the tre-

mendous political power of Senator Robert A. Taft of Ohio. No one denied Taft's integrity and ability. But they believed that he did not have sufficient popularity to defeat the Democrats. And even if elected, they felt he would owe so much to the reactionary and neo-isolationist elements in his party that he would be forced to follow their views. They feared that such an administration would weaken American leadership of the free world. Mamie knew that Ike thought so too.

Throughout the rainy autumn of 1951, Mamie watched Ike worry about what was the right thing to do. On the one hand his job at SHAPE, though well begun, was only half completed. On the other, the election of an administration hostile to American participation in European affairs might wreck the whole edifice of international cooperation. At times Mamie yearned over her troubled husband with an almost maternal desire to soothe him. But true to her principles she would make no move to sway his decision. For she did not feel competent to judge the issue. She could only hope—in secret— that he would refuse. It was strictly up to Ike.

In the end, Ike chose the harder course. On January 7, 1952, he announced, in effect, that he was a candidate for the Republican nomination for President of the United States.

Mamie had been sure he would all along.

26

Eisenhower Special

MAMIE'S DETERMINATION TO STAY IN THE BACKGROUND
worked well enough until Ike came home to fight for the
Republican nomination and the presidency. Then she
found that to help him she must be on the front page as
much as possible. The more .publicity she got—good
publicity that is—the better it was for him.

She took a very pessimistic view of her capability in
this direction. At SHAPE, after her unhappy experience
with the French press, she had been more retiring than
ever. Reports of the visits of star-studded celebrities to
Marnes La Coquette always spoke of them as going to
see General Eisenhower. Though Mamie was there, making them feel at home in her open-hearted fashion, you
would never have known it by reading the papers.

This reached such a point that Eileen Archibold, who
knew the political ropes, having been Republican Na-

tional Committeewoman from Colorado, wrote to Mamie asking, "Where were you when Princess Margaret Rose came? If you are going to help Ike, you must get into the picture." To which Mamie replied, "I will try, but you know me. Ha! Ha!"

Mamie's baptism of fire came on June 4, 1952, when Ike went back to Abilene to open the preconvention campaign with the first political speech he had ever made. He had refused to say a word until his formal retirement from the Army in Washington the day before. For Mamie that first day was the worst—and in some ways the best.

As the long, silver, special train rolled down the home stretch from Chapman to Abilene, Mamie's insides felt like inferior calf's-foot jelly. This was the real test of her ability to help Ike in his new career. She tried to tell herself that she had passed other exams successfully. She knew that she had done all right in Quarters One and in Europe. But somehow generals and statesmen and royalty had never made her as nervous as this. Always before there had been the cushion of conventional courtesy—people who met you on formal occasions had to be polite whether they liked you or not. But this was politics with no sissy trimmings, and the People with a capital P had the final say. If they liked you, fine; if they did not, you knew it quick enough.

The train pulled up alongside of a platform specially built at the spot where the Eisenhower back lot abutted on the tracks of the Union Pacific. Holding tight to Ike's arm, Mamie stepped out of the air-conditioned car into the sticky heat of a thunderstormy Kansas day, and a roar of sound that you felt you could lean on. There were quick greetings to old friends on the platform, and hasty introductions to smiling, weatherbeaten men who looked like farmers because they mostly were.

The first ceremony was laying the cornerstone of the museum to be built by the Eisenhower Foundation adjoining the house where Ike grew up. As Mamie walked beside him along a boardwalk between smiling, friendly faces, she suddenly realized that some of the cheers were for her, that the crowd seemed to like her too. Her nervousness disappeared in a glow of friendliness.

When they mounted the dais, there was another wild ovation. This was not the occasion of the real speech, which would come later. Ike talked very simply about his boyhood and the fine things his father and mother had stood for. Mamie could tell that he was tremendously moved. He kept looking at the familiar yard with verbena and sweetpeas blooming, and red roses climbing up the back porch. Then Ike knelt down to put the cement under the cornerstone with a silver trowel. When he stood up, Mamie saw that his eyes were full of tears.

It was silly of him to be so sentimental. So, of course, she cried too.

After that they went through the small-town streets, jammed with country folk from all over the state, to the Sunflower Hotel, where their suite of two tiny rooms was soon packed with people come to greet Ike. That was where Mamie learned that the phrase, "smoke-filled room," was no mere figure of speech.

The opening-gun speech was set for five o'clock at the baseball park. It came close to being a misfire. As they drove out, thunderheads towered above them, and the western sky was plum-purple shot with lightening gold. About five minutes before the zero hour the storm broke in the full fury of lashing rain, wind, and the ear-splitting crack of lightning striking close. For once, the Eisenhower luck was out.

There was no shelter, and no chance of postponement. Forty million people or more, in all the states and territories of the Union, were sitting by their radios and television sets waiting to hear Ike. He could not disappoint them. In a borrowed hat Ike stepped onto the platform draped with sodden bunting, and began trying to shout down the elements.

Mamie, her hat and dress a watery wreck, sat with clenched teeth, so intent on Ike's performance that she hardly noticed her own misery. It was amazing how many people stayed to hear him: women in mud-splattered summer finery, men with their trousers rolled up to their knees. Ike had rolled his trousers up too. His voice was clear and firm between the crackles of static. When a thunderbolt drowned him out, he went back and said it again. Part of the time his rain-blurred spectacles failed him, and he talked from memory or spontaneously said what came to mind.

The speech was magnificent on the field, but not very good over the air waves. The wonder is that it was made at all.

From Abilene they went to Denver, where at least half the shouting was for Mamie. As they came by the corner of Colfax Avenue on their way to the Douds, she saw a sheet held up between broomsticks on which was printed:

LAFAYETTE STREET GANG

says

WELCOME MAMIE!

Eisenhower headquarters were set up in the famous old Brown Palace Hotel, which looked like a huge chocolate flatiron. It was built around a central well ten stories high from the lobby to the roof, with balconies running around it at every floor. The headquarters were a rabbit warren of rooms on the mezzanine, and the Eisenhowers also had the large presidential suite on the top floor, though they mostly slept at home on Lafayette Street—when they had time to sleep at all.

To Mamie's amazement all the politicians and delegates, newspaper people, and influential amateurs seemed to want to meet her as well as Ike. Mostly she received them in the long flower-filled drawing room of the suite. If she happened to be at home when a fresh delegation arrived, Arthur Vandenberg would send a hurry call, and Mamie would dress and get down to the Brown like a fireman going down a brass pole.

At other times people would come to Lafayette Street, and Mamie would sit on the red carpet and talk to them;

she liked that way best. She did not talk about politics at all. Not thinking she knew enough, she stuck to her old theory of letting Ike run the office. So she just chatted about things in general or showed her visitors pictures of her grandchildren—there were three of them now: David, Barbara Ann, and the new baby, Susan, whom she called "Susy Q." Though she did not realize it, this was very good politics.

Sometimes Ike went off on speech-making trips. The time for the Republican convention was getting close and the fight for the nomination was red hot. Senator Taft had many more delegates pledged to him than Ike could count on, and acted sure of winning. A lot of people in the Eisenhower camp were pretty despondent. Mamie did not worry. Her solution for all the ills of the world was to elect Ike President, and she felt sure inside herself that the people would do it.

When the time came to leave for the convention in Chicago, Mamie had developed a fierce neuralgic headache. It felt like a toothache in her temple. Ordinarily she would have taken to her bed, but she had no time for such nonsense. General Snyder filled her full of aspirin and other pain killers to keep her going.

The group on the train with Mamie and Ike were a close-knit band of adventurers in the political arena. Lodge was already in Chicago corralling delegates, and with the exception of Senator Carlson and solid, hard-working Arthur Vandenberg, they were mostly amateurs, challenging the great professionals of the Taft machine. There were the idealist young men of Citizens for Eisenhower; devoted secretaries like Ann Whitman and Ann Wheaton; businessmen who had given up their profitable time to the cause, and a group of young people who cheerfully ran errands. They were like blood brothers, devoted to each other and their general. Mamie called them all by their first names, and half the time they called her Mamie.

The Eisenhower Special made a triumphal progress. Every place it stopped crowds were cheering and Mamie always managed to get out to wave and smile as happily as though her head were not ready to crack. In Chicago they went to the Blackstone Hotel. Then the pressure really came on.

As the delegates poured into the city, it seemed as if every one of them wanted to meet Eisenhower whether they intended to vote for him or not. After they saw Ike, they wanted to meet Mamie. They came through the suite in droves all day and most of the night. Somehow Mamie seemed to be able to make them feel like old friends in five minutes. Whenever anybody started to talk about the business at hand, she always said, "I don't understand politics." But after watching delegation after delegation go solemn and tight-lipped into Mamie's room and come out laughing in evident delight, a newspaperman told her, "You're the best politician of the lot."

Senator Carlson acted as her mentor in political nuances, and she learned a good deal more than she admitted. During the frantic first days of the convention, she came to understand the meaning of the moves and countermoves on the seating of rival delegations; the importance of whether Ike's most powerful friend, Governor Dewey, could hold most of New York's 96 delegates for Eisenhower, and the significance of the close votes on controversial changes in the rules. When the convention was in session, her radio was always on, or she watched it on the TV set in the parlor.

It was all black and white to her. The people for Ike were heroes and those for Taft were villains or else terribly misguided. Indeed, in the heat and fury of those final days this was pretty much the point of view of everybody in both camps with the exception of the principals. Both Eisenhower and Taft managed to keep sane enough to believe that the Union would not totter even if their rival were nominated.

Came the morning of the first vote on the candidates. Eisenhower headquarters were a wild confusion of men either shouting loudly or whispering in corners. Mamie was flat on her back with the worst headache yet. It was eased a bit by General Snyder's ministrations, but she had a feeling of floating in unreality.

When the convention was called to order, things quieted down in Eisenhower's suite. The general, Mrs. Doud and a few close friends sat in the parlor watching it on television. Mamie lay in bed with the radio on, while Snyder kept track of the votes on a tally sheet. "Alabama, 14 votes," came the chairman's resonant voice; and the echo from the floor, "Alabama votes for Taft. . . ."

As the states voted in alphabetical order, Taft piled up a big early lead. Then Governor Dewey brought in a thundering 92 votes out of New York's total of 96, and Ike forged ahead. Mamie lost track of the counting, but Snyder kept telling her the totals. Lesser candidates like Governor Earl Warren of California and Harold Stassen of Minnesota were picking up a few votes. It became evident that Ike would not get the 604 votes needed for a clear majority on the first ballot. As the final vote, that of the Virgin Islands, was counted, Snyder said, "Ike's got 595 votes, nine short of a majority."

"Does that mean we're beaten?" Mamie asked.

"No. Taft only has 500. It's good. Wait a minute—"

Out of the confused jumble of sound from the convention floor a voice was calling. The chairman's bellow cut through the babel. "Does Minnesota wish to change its vote?" (Minnesota had cast 19 votes for Stassen.)

"Yes," came the far-off voice. "Minnesota votes for Eisenhower."

"That does it!" said General Snyder.

Then it seemed lots of states wanted to change their votes; the stampede to Eisenhower was on.

Ike came quickly into the room and sat down on Mamie's bed. With a protective instinct she said vaguely, "Honey, everything's going to be all right!"

Ike's grin flashed for a second, "I know," he said.

Then he took her hand and sat there thinking hard. Suddenly he stood up decisively and said, "I'm going right across the street to see Senator Taft."

That was so like him, Mamie thought, to go straight to the defeated candidate instead of waiting, as protocol demanded, for Taft to come to him. He would begin healing the wounds right away, so that the Republicans could fight the election as a united party. But Mamie also knew that it was not just a political move; Ike was not that subtle. It was his instinctive generosity toward a valiant, though vanquished, opponent.

That night Mamie went with Ike to the convention for his acceptance speech. Guarded by secret-service men, who took over when Eisenhower was nominated, they drove through the cheering crowds to the convention hall. The place was riotous. Secret-service men, friends, and even strangers formed a flying wedge around them and fought through the tight-packed tumultous throng. It took nearly ten minutes to reach the comparative security of the platform.

And what of Mamie's terror of crowds? How did she survive? "Survive, heck! I loved it!" Her headache had vanished and she stood radiant in the dazzling television lights, laughing and waving, while such cheers as she had never heard before beat against them until sound seemed to defeat itself and the uproar became an elemental condition of life. When it stopped, at last, the silence was almost ear-splitting.

Of course, Mamie cried a little as Ike solemnly and humbly accepted the nomination. Then she was laughing again, calling out to friends, as the flying wedge formed up to carry them out to the car. It had been an incredible day. Victory was so complete that it was hard for Mamie to realize that it was just a preliminary skirmish. The real fight for the Presidency had not even begun. . . .

They all flew back to Denver for ten days' rest. Ike went fishing in the mountains, and Mamie went to bed and pretty much stayed there. Meanwhile the Democrats had their day in Chicago and nominated Adlai Stevenson. According to Ike, they had picked their best man. It was going to be a hard fight.

Headquarters was reactivated at the Brown Palace, but there were lots of changes; for now it was the center of the whole Republican party. To make room for Taftites in the interest of harmony, some of the early stalwarts like Lodge, Dewey, and Duff withdrew to the background. In their place came Senator Fred A. Seton of Nebraska, a brisk and dapper, businessman-in-politics, and Congressman Clifford Hope, an old timer from Kansas. Governor Sherman Adams of New Hampshire, a wiry little Yankee, headed the organization.

To Mamie's great delight, Senator Carlson stayed with them, and their good friend from Columbia days, Kevin McCann, was there, rambling through the rooms doing every needed job from advising on high policy to licking envelopes. Another pillar of support was Press Secretary James C. Hagerty, a temperamental Irishman who was always frantic and, paradoxically, completely efficient. Being a newspaperman himself and the son of a great political reporter, Jim Hagerty could handle "the boys" like nobody else.

As soon as Ike got back from his fishing trip, they all plunged into the work of organizing the campaign. Mamie stayed with Ike at the hotel now—there was no time to go to the Douds except on Sundays. They both got up at six every morning, and were hard at work before eight. The amount of mail Mamie got amazed her— about 300 letters a day. She answered them all with the help of her new chief secretary, Mary Jane McCaffree, and Ann Wheaton.

Almost all the letters were friendly, but quite a few of them from women urged Mamie to do away with her bangs. When anybody mentioned the bangs to her in person, she had a way of sweeping them back showing that her hair line was almost an inch higher than the average. "You've got to cover it somehow," she would say, "and, besides, Ike likes my bangs." That settled that.

People who thought that Ike would jitter and Mamie wilt under the pressure of politics could not have been more mistaken. They both thrived on it. General Snyder summed it up by saying, "Ike's bitten the bullet. He's in it heart and soul, and actually enjoying it." Snyder's diagnosis was also true of Mamie.

She even learned to handle things by herself. For example, when Ike was off speech-making, the vice-presidential nominee, Senator Richard M. Nixon, came to Denver. It was up to Mamie to entertain him. Her first move was to telephone Colorado's genial, cowboy-booted governor, Dan Thornton, "I'm giving a party for the Nixons, please help me out by playing host."

"Of course," said Governor Dan, immensely pleased and flattered.

"Do you think he'll like a party in our back yard?"

"He's sure to."

It was a fine party, with barbecued steak, corn roasted in the embers, and watermelon. Thornton had been one of Eisenhower's strongest supporters; he became Mamie's ardent fan. "I was working sixteen hours a day and really beaten down," he said. "Then I'd see Mamie and come away refreshed. It was a new day."

Another time when Mamie went it alone was much later at a meeting of Republican women in St. Louis. Somehow arrangements had gone awry; there was no one to introduce her, no one even in charge. As two hundred leaderless women pushed around her, Mamie took command. In a clear, authoritative voice that surprised her, she shouted, "Form in line! If you form in line, I'll be glad to shake hands with all of you."

The restoration of order that followed seemed miraculous to her.

Such action would have been unthinkable for Mamie a year, or even two months before. You can hear her, had it been suggested, saying, "You know me. Ha, Ha!"

Mamie was not always so politically sure-footed. In

Denver she nearly wrecked the local Republican women's setup when she yielded to the persuasion of the Douds' old Negro cook, Jerusha, to attend a meeting of her particular Republican club, and forgot to notify the strategists at Ike's headquarters. Since that was the only women's meeting she went to in Denver, other organizations were foaming with rage. Mamie found that impulsive kindness was apt to boomerang.

There was one bad day in Denver that had nothing to do with politics. That was when John flew in on his way to Korea. Late in the evening Mamie went out to the air base where they had set aside a room in which she could be with her son for a few precious minutes. She had been a good soldier's wife, but her fortitude was not quite equal to saying good-by to John. She broke down like a million other mothers. When she came out her face was swollen and tear-streaked in the merciless glare of the photographers' flash bulbs that pursued her even there.

But she was more determined than ever that Ike must be President. With supreme confidence she told herself, "He'll either win that darn war or stop it somehow."

Early in September Eisenhower headquarters were moved to the Commodore Hotel in New York, while Ike and Mamie went to live at 60 Morningside Drive. It was both familiar and strange to be in the big house again, at home but not really home. At any rate, she did not have time to settle in before she was off on the campaign train.

The first trip of the Eisenhower Special was scheduled to run through twelve Western and Southern states, while Ike made eight major speeches and 77 whistle-stop talks.

Actually there were many more. Mamie frankly dreaded
the trip, but like everything else that had worried her
about this strange adventure, it turned out to be quite
wonderful. Speaking in retrospect, she says, "The campaign train was wearing, but so rewarding that I would
not give up the memory of it for anything. The wonderful faces we saw all over the country, so happy and
contented! It was inspiring because, you see, we had
been away so long from people who looked happy."

Even train life has a routine, and Mamie soon got
into the swing of it. Up early in the morning; breakfast
with wives of the local politicos while the men talked
politics; then a stop at some city, and the motorcade
through the roaring streets, with Mamie sitting on a
couple of cushions in the back of a convertible waving
and yelling "Hi!" to shouts of "Hi, Mamie." Then the
speech; a short reception; the rush back to the train; a
whistle stop with Ike talking seriously from the rear
platform, and finally saying, "Now I want you to meet
Mamie," and beckoning her to come out. Mamie would
kid with the crowd and lean over to sign autographs.
Then the train would pull out, and they'd do it all over
again half an hour later. The pattern varied from state
to state and day to day, but in the main that is how it
went.

One stop that was not even a whistle stop became famous throughout the nation. Just at dawn the train pulled
up beside a shedlike station in the sparse pine woods of
North Carolina. Two or three hundred people who had
risen in the dead of night in the hope of a glimpse of
the Eisenhowers, crowded around the car.

Ike, in his dressing gown came into Mamie's state-
room. "Come on, Honey! Let's say hello to them!"

"Like this?" asked Mamie.

"Sure! You're pretty as a picture."

So, in her robe, with her hair in curlers, Mamie went to the car door and stood with Ike laughing with the friendly people. A reporter who was in the crowd told her that he heard one woman say, *"She's* going to get him elected." It made Mamie very proud.

Incidentally, the picture that was taken then appeared in virtually every newspaper and undoubtedly brought in a lot of votes. By that picture also hangs a tale. There were three press-association photographers on the train, representing AP, UP and INS. Only one of them had taken the trouble to get up for that dawn stop, and he got the picture of a lifetime. A little later, while Mamie was having breakfast, Jim Hagerty came in and explained the situation. "The other two boys are in bad trouble," he said. "They're apt to get fired."

"We can fix that," Mamie said. "I'll put my hair up in curlers again, and we'll restage it." (And they did.)

In October the Eisenhowers took the train again up through New England. The Yankees seemed just as hotly enthusiastic as the Westerners and Southerners. But the politicians told Mamie that it was far from a sure thing. The public opinion polls gave Eisenhower a slight lead, but the polls were apt to err in favor of the Republicans. Ike was radiantly confident. Mamie proudly watched him getting better at his new job every day.

The final days were a sort of blur. The huge rally in Madison Square Garden, and Election Eve in Boston's Garden with a rally followed by the television-radio broadcast when the Eisenhowers and Nixons appeared together informally. Ike said the last word just at midnight in an impromptu speech.

As they went down to the waiting car, Mamie said, "That was a beautiful speech, Ike."

Ike smiled his pleasure. "Was it, truly?" he asked. And then, vaguely, "What did I say?"

Election Day was surprisingly peaceful. The train got to New York just as daylight began to filter through the city haze. Mamie and Ike, who had three hours of dubious sleep, drove straight to the polling place. They voted at 7:38 A.M., the straight Republican ticket. Then they went to 60 Morningside for a long, lazy day. Mamie mostly slept and Ike painted a little. They had the peaceful feeling that everything had been done that they could do.

About six that evening they went up to the sun porch on the roof, where the television set stood. Mamma Doud was there as well as Barbara and the children. A few very close friends came in, among them the Snyders and the Nevins. Art Nevins was rather red-faced because his brother Allen had declared for Stevenson. Ike laughed it off: "A man's got to vote the way he feels is right."

By eight o'clock the returns were pouring in. Mamie could hardly believe them, they sounded so good. The wise ones scattered grains of salt—"too early to tell anything." But the news got better. The soldier vote was going to Ike two to one. By eight-thirty Connecticut had gone for Eisenhower. He was leading almost everywhere. Even the solid South was cracking: Eisenhower led in Virginia 48,000 to 34,000; he was leading in Florida! As the farm states of the Midwest came in, the trend was confirmed. Mamie's eyes were shining. Although she had always known that Ike was wonderful, it was thrilling to see the whole country putting its confidence in him.

By 10:00 P.M., when they started for election headquarters, they knew that Ike had won. In the roaring rooms at the Hotel Commodore, the next two hours went by in bedlam. Then Adlai Stevenson made a graceful speech conceding Eisenhower's victory. At 2:00 A.M. Mamie walked with her husband into the packed ballroom of the Commodore, and the blaze of the television lights, for Ike's quietly humble victory speech. "Let us unite for the better future of America for our children and our grandchildren. . . . We cannot now do all the job ahead of us except as a united people. . . ."

As they rode homeward through Central Park, with the motorcycle escort sputtering around them, Ike and Mamie were almost as silent and solemn as if they had lost. They were both thinking of their respective jobs ahead; each in his own way. Eisenhower was both inspired and oppressed by the awful responsibility of the American people's confidence in him, and the question of how he could serve them best. Mamie, sharply personal in her point of view, thought only of how she could best help Ike.

27

A Prayer at Noon

To MOST AMERICANS THE PRESIDENCY IS NOT SYMBOL-
ized by a flag, or an eagle holding a claw full of lightning, or any other official trappings. Just as the dome of
the Capitol is the trade-mark of democracy, the White
House stands for the chief executive. Its beauty and dignity fit the prestige of the office, but it is not at all forbidding. Indeed, its columned portico suggests the
hospitality that since pioneer times has been a cherished
national trait, and its very name implies the simplicity
that is expected of its occupant despite the power he
wields.

Mamie Eisenhower shared the national feeling of
respect and affection for the White House. She knew that
while she lived there she would become part of its tradition. To a person with her fondness for informality it
was both shattering and humorous to think of herself as

a symbol. She did not feel in the least like a bald eagle or even the Queen of England, but since it seemed that her position would be slightly akin to both; she proposed to act the part in the finest tradition of the White House. At the same time she was quite ferociously determined to make it a home for herself and Ike.

The first step was a personally conducted tour of the house by Mrs. Truman. Mamie wasted very little time on the state rooms on the ground floor. She knew them well enough, and, besides, there was nothing she could do about them since they were under the direction of the Fine Arts Commission. However, she did cast a sharp eye over the shiny new electrified kitchen with a view toward convenience and economy; for she was acutely aware that several Presidents had gone into their capital running this place and she did not propose to let Ike do that.

It was the second floor that interested Mamie most. Here she could exercise her talent for homemaking, although with tourists pouring through the lower floors every week day from 10:00 A.M. to noon she would feel a little like a pigeon nest-building in the New York Public Library.

In rather less than half an hour, Mamie had the whole thing planned out as she mentally shifted furniture around. There were not nearly enough closets so she decided to make Mrs. Truman's small southwest corner bedroom into a dressing room, taking the larger sitting room next door to sleep in. The outsize double bed, which she had made to order for Quarters One, would fit against the west wall with one of Ike's landscapes over it. In another corner there was room for the wonderful old desk with a complete bed that popped out of it, which she had inherited from Grandma Carlson.

Ike would have a large connecting room for his dressing room; and their sitting room would be the closed-off end of the broad corridor that ran the full length of the house.

Mamie decided to have her bedroom painted the color she liked best, light green; there must be painters on the payroll who could do that at no great expense. Since her bed was her favorite shade of pink, the rest of the furniture had to be in accord. As she went through the other rooms, Mamie kept her eyes out for pink pieces she could borrow for her bedroom. The draperies in Margaret Truman's room on the north side matched exactly; she would take them and save the government the expense of getting new drapes. She picked a room directly across the hall for Mrs. Doud, who would be here a good deal, she hoped.

Decorating the President's Oval Study would be up to Ike, with a few tactful suggestions, of course. Mamie, a confirmed porch-sitter, liked the balcony outside it that President Truman had built despite the row about it. Later she and Ike were often grateful to escape from the air-conditioned sterility of their rooms and sit there enjoying the grass-sweet evening breeze from the river.

Farther along the hall was the Lincoln Room, where the Emancipation Proclamation had been signed. Though his extra-long, carved bed was there now, Mamie knew that President Lincoln had used it as his office, and had slept in the room she was planning for her own. With a dutiful historical gasp she passed on—the Lincoln Room was a case of "best not to touch."

In the Rose Suite, traditional quarters of visiting

royalty, the huge four-poster bed was very high off the ground. Mamie made a mental note to have some sort of steps built for it—if the tiny queen of England ever came visiting, she would never make the grade.

On the third floor, Mamie was mainly interested in accommodations for her grandchildren. There was a suite of rooms where they could put in a kitchenette to prepare the children's food. The playroom was pretty small but she guessed it would do. . . .

As Mamie came out on the portico with Mrs. Truman, the photographers rushed up. A reporter looked at the beautiful fur coat Ike had given her when he sold *Crusade*. "What's that coat made of?" he asked.

Mamie knew the reference was to Nixon's campaign phrase about "a good Republican cloth coat." She grinned and said airily, "Mink, of course."

Talking her new quarters over with her sister Mike, who now lived on Klingle Street out Connecticut Avenue way, Mamie was enthusiastic. The spacious rooms, with their graceful classic furniture and sunshine pouring

through the windows, gave one a sense of serenity which was as agreeable as it was unexpected. Despite the responsibilities that weighed upon its occupants, she felt that the White House was a happy place.

According to inflexible tradition the Trumans must move out of the White House and the Eisenhowers move in between speeches on Inauguration Day. In all her many moves Mamie had never faced one that was quite like this. To take everything out of 60 Morningside, where she would never live in again, and move into a place two hundred miles away in about 24 hours was a problem in logistics that might have baffled even Ike. It took extremely careful planning and split-second timing. She spent the next six weeks—mostly sitting up in bed with a heavy cold—organizing the arrangements. They worked as well as the plans for D day.

When she was not working on her moving day, Mamie was assembling a First Lady's wardrobe. She bought some very expensive dresses, among them a gray dressmaker suit from Hattie Carnegie to wear at the Inauguration ceremonies. She made that eminent *couturière* redesign the skirt so it was very full, the way she always liked it. Her sparkling, pink, bouffant-skirted ball gown was from Nettie Rosenstein via Neiman-Marcus; there were daytime and evening dresses by Mollie Parnis, and a couple of dozen Sally Victor hats, all small and close-fitting.

In addition, there were many inexpensive dresses, which Mamie had picked up in her travels. She loves a bargain and does not care where a dress comes from so long as it suits her. Once from a roaring motorcade in the campaign, she saw a dress in a shop window for

$39.95, which she knew was just what she needed. She made a careful mental note of the store, wrote back and ordered it. Like all Army wives Mamie had been a mail-order addict. Now that she could no longer go shopping without a great hullabaloo, she reverted to her former habit.

The Eisenhowers spent the night before the Inaugural in the suite at the Statler which they had occupied for a few hours the day Ike came home from the war. Mamie woke up early and looked anxiously out of the window. It was Eisenhower weather, all right, with rosy sunlight tinting the buildings and air as soft as April. She ordered a pot of coffee and some toast. Then she dressed for the special service at the National Presbyterian Church, putting on the gray suit and a small white hat that was a present from a Virginian lady she had never met. There were 34 members of the Eisenhower and Doud families at the church—Mrs. Doud, John and Barbara, of course; all of Ike's brothers and their wives; Mike and her husband; the Joel Carlsons, and cousins from all over the country.

Back at the Statler, Mamie changed her hat to a gray, close-fitting Sally Victor and freshened her make-up. It was nearly time to pick up the Trumans, when Ike, in shirt sleeves, came barging through the connecting door. "Say, Mamie," he said, "do you think it would be all right if I say a prayer?"

"A prayer?" Mamie asked.

"At the ceremony. Before my speech."

Mamie smiled fondly at his earnestness. "It's always a good thing to say a prayer," she answered softly.

It was then that Ike called a secretary, and, standing

beside Mamie's dressing table, dictated the moving prayer that was his first official utterance as President of the United States.

Washington was like a county fair that day. Everyone wore a smile and even the delays caused by the jostling crowds were taken in good spirits. Mamie rode with Mrs. Truman and Margaret down Pennsylvania Avenue between the massed tiers of cheering people. When she came out on the platform built on the Capitol steps, the great square in front of her was filled with gaily dressed people as far as she could see.

The simple, beautiful ceremony in which the enormous power of the presidency was transferred from one man to another took so brief a time that Mamie hardly realized when it was over and her husband was President of the United States.

The President's first act was as surprising as it was characteristic. As soon as he had spoken the last solemn words of the Oath of Office, Ike strode quickly over to Mamie and kissed her.

After that there were a few moments of happy confusion. Mamie was laughing and crying at the same time, as the smiling dignitaries offered congratulations. Then the new President walked to the rostrum, and in the utter silence of the great reverent crowd spoke the humble prayer he had written that morning in Mamie's dressing room.

Every previous President had driven back from the Capitol to the White House with his vice-president. Right here Ike broke another precedent. Mamie rode beside him in the open car while the Nixons followed in another. The solemnity of the Inaugural ceremony was gone. Ike was grinning his broadest, and Mamie sparkling with happiness. As they reached the stands in front of the White House, Ike shouted and pointed to his old friends sitting there. Mamie smiled and kissed her hand in greeting.

The Eisenhowers went directly to their place in the President's box. There they perched on stool-like, high chairs to review the great parade. It was a long ordeal, five hours long, but Mamie would not have missed a moment of it. For that parade was America at its wonderful, homey best; not grim or grand like the massed troops solemnly stalking by the rulers of less favored nations; but alive with the color, vitality, and, above all, the good humor that are our especial national characteristics. Even the cowboy, who asked permission to rope the President and then failed at the first attempt, added a congruous note. Where else in all the world would a man who wields such awful power as Ike does, permit such tomfoolery? Somehow it seemed to prove that despite our vast responsibilities and our terrible armaments, exemplified in the grim atomic cannon lumbering through the gathering dusk, we still kept our national sense of humor.

It was 7:02 P.M. and full night when Mamie walked with Ike up to the great columned portico of her new home. John Mays, who had served every President since William Howard Taft, swung the door wide open for them. Was there in his straight, slender figure, his somehow touching dignity, something reminiscent of Tall and Stately Jack of long ago?

"Good evening, Mr. President. Good evening, Mrs. Eisenhower," he said.

Smiling happily, Mamie crossed the threshold of the White House, holding tightly to her husband's arm.

AFTERWORD

First Lady

Since mamie is still in the white house, where it looks as though she might stay rather longer than in any of her other numerous homes, no definite picture of her as First Lady should be attempted. However, her manner on each different occasion, from the dignified camaraderie of her way with the D.A.R. to the mighty sideswipe with which she burst the bottle of champagne on the stubby bow of the *Nautilus,* shows that she took the job in her stride.

She needed only one day to rest up from the rigors of the Inaugural and its twin balls. That day the house was full of family, and she visited with her folks. She let John and Barbara sleep in the royal grandeur of the Rose Suite the first night, just for the fun of it.

On the second day, Mamie settled into her routine and took the reins of management into her strong slender hands. She had been better trained than most President's wives for the executive side of her job, for she had run many houses staffed by government employees, as is the White House.

Of course, the Eisenhowers brought their own personal staff, including Bob Schulz as military aide, Bill Draper of the Air Force and Mary Jane McCaffree as Mamie's personal and social secretary, assisted by Ann Wheaton. To look after the Eisenhowers' comfort, there was Rose Wood and Sergeant Moany and his wife Delores.

That second day half-began for Mamie when, before dawn, Sergeant Moany called softly at the door to wake the President, who slipped quietly out of bed. At eight Rose came in with Mamie's usual meager breakfast. Then Chief Usher Howell G. Crimm arrived to check appointments followed by Mrs. Mabel C. Walker to talk over the meals. It is not true that Mamie just approves the menus. She says that she actually orders all the meals whether it is supper for two, which she and President Ike may have served in front of the TV set, or a state dinner. She even plans the food for Ike's stag luncheons and dinners, for she knows very well what men like to eat.

In fact, Mamie runs two households: the Eisenhowers' own, which includes their family and personal guests, and is paid for by the President, and the state establishment for official entertainment chargeable to the government. While Mamie never skimps, she is shrewdly economical as Pooh Bah taught her to be, and as careful with government funds as with her own.

After the ordering was done, Mary Jane McCaffree came in with the morning mail, hundreds of letters. While she works with Mrs. McCaffree, Mamie stays in bed to conserve her strength; besides, lying late abed is an old Denver custom. If there are no duties or appointments to interrupt them they sometimes keep hard at it until late afternoon, for Mamie tries to give everyone who writes a satisfactory answer. Just as in Denver, when she piled Creepy full of squirmy little boys, she is a soft touch for children. Their letters are always answered and sometimes an invitation to the White House is included.

There are also hundreds of beautiful and curious presents to be acknowledged, ranging all the way from a small rag doll with Mamie bangs, which she loved, to a whole hog on ice. Perhaps the present which touched her most was a sampler painstakingly stitched with the President's Inaugural Prayer.

Of course, on most days the letter answering is interrupted by official engagements or receptions for anywhere up to a couple of thousand women. Mamie's record for handshaking almost equals that set by energetic Mrs. Franklin D. Roosevelt—Mamie knows that it is a good way to help Ike.

In the evening there may be one of the state dinners, with Mamie and Ike sitting side by side in big carved chairs at the huge glittering table with ninety to a hundred distinguished guests in their best clothes and party manners. Mamie found that these affairs were pretty glacial despite anything she could do. An example is the dinner for the President of Turkey, where conversation was totally limited by the fact that the Turk spoke no English, nobody else understood Turkish, and no interpreter was present.

Sometimes, though, Mamie broke protocol wide open. There was the time when Governors Allen Shivers of

Texas and Dan Thornton of Colorado came in from playing golf with Ike at the Burning Tree Club. While they sat chatting with the President in the sitting room, Mamie came in dressed for a formal dinner. Then, while the President dressed, she insisted on showing them over the White House, ending up in the children's rooms on the third floor.

After the tour, she escorted them down the main stairway. As Governor Dan describes it, they came around the turn, and found the great hall filled with people in white ties, tails, and ball gowns, their jewels and decorations out-glittering the crystal chandeliers. "There we were," says Governor Dan, "in sport shirts, old pants and cowboy boots, all dirty and sweaty from our game. We actually turned pale.

" 'Let's ease out a back way,' suggested Shivers.

" 'No you don't,' said Mamie.

"She put an arm around each of us and marched us into the Blue Room, saying, 'Folks, I want you to meet my two Western governors.' "

After that Mamie practically owned Texas and Colorado. Governor Shivers summed it up by saying, "There can't be a situation that this First Lady can't handle."

Governor Dan said, "She reminds me of Dolly Madison."

On the lucky evenings when they do not have to work at their job, the Eisenhowers like to have supper on trays, and, perhaps, invite some of their old friends in for a movie or a bridge game. Quite often they end up singing while Mamie plays the Hammond electric organ that Mrs. Doud gave her for a birthday present. The organ is one of Mamie's chief recreations in the White

House; she practices almost daily and has recaptured her youthful touch. Ike still loves to sing—off key.

Occasionally Mamie gets Ruth Butcher, Mrs. Walker, Mrs. Snyder, Ann Nevins, or others of her old friends to come in the afternoon for a game of Bolivia, which is to canasta what contract is to bridge whist.

Except that the pressures are greater, Mamie says that she does not find the business of First Ladying so very different from the way she has lived ever since Ike came home from the war. She has her public life and her private life, and never the twain shall meet, if she can help it. A symptom of this is the way she jealously defends the privacy of her sacred second floor. Anyone who gets up there is a real friend of the family. From her lair in the East Executive Wing, Mary Jane McCaffree guards Mamie's privacy like a well-bred tigress.

Mamie had a lot of fun fixing up the farm at Gettysburg for their eventual retirement. Her enthusiasm for decorating houses partly stems from frustration at never having had one of her own, and partly is due to her confidence in doing a good job. The vacation cottage at the Augusta National Golf Club afforded another exercise for her talent. Naturally the interior is harmonized around Mamie's favorite shades of green and pink.

On their trip to Denver last summer the Eisenhowers were almost able to go back in time to welcome anonymity. Once again Mamie sat on the red carpet and entertained her friends, while Ike roamed the lower slopes of the Rockies catching outsize trout and came home to grill a steak in the back yard.

Back in Washington, Mamie, slipping into the White House routine of two lives, found it agreeably familiar.

She even enjoyed the public occasions, feeling the sense of accomplishment of a thing worth doing done well. Besides she still likes meeting people. Her private life was as happy as could be, with her grandchildren frequent visitors, and her friends dropping in.

One day Mike came by with a box of bits of black courtplaster cut in the shapes of hearts and crescents and stars.

"I found these beauty spots rummaging through your old dressing table," she told Mamie. "Remember how you used always to wear them when you were the belle of Denver?"

"Sure," said Mamie. "They were real becoming."

She took one from the box and stuck it just below her left cheekbone. "Pretty snazzy," she said, admiring herself in the mirror on her dressing table. "Golly, I'd like to wear this to the state dinner tonight!"

Her eyes sparkled as she toyed with the idea. "I suppose it wouldn't be dignified," she decided reluctantly, "but it sure would start a fad."

That was Mamie of Lafayette Street, who could laugh at anything, including herself, but who always could do what she had to do for Ike. The glittering big-wigs who stand waiting in the stately rooms on the lower floor see her playing her part to the hilt. The Marine Corps band blares out "Hail to the Chief" in splendid diapason. The President and Mrs. Eisenhower walk slowly down the great stairway. She is dressed in as exquisite a creation as the imagination of woman—or man—can devise. The sheen of glamour is on her, and the dignity of her great position too.

But her friends like best to think of her as she receives

them when they drop in on her of a morning, sitting bolt upright in her vast pink bed, wearing a dainty pink negligee and a pink satin bow in her hair, her blue eyes sparkling with fun of it all, in the room where Lincoln slept.

Index